T0330361

FINANCIAL INCLUSION
Critique and Alternatives

Rajiv Prabhakar

First published in Great Britain in 2021 by

Policy Press, an imprint of
Bristol University Press
University of Bristol
1–9 Old Park Hill
Bristol
BS2 8BB
UK
t: +44 (0)117 954 5940
e: bup-info@bristol.ac.uk

Details of international sales and distribution partners are available at:
policy.bristoluniversitypress.co.uk

© Bristol University Press 2021

British Library Cataloguing in Publication Data
A catalogue record for this book is available from the British Library

ISBN 978-1-4473-4546-6 hardcover
ISBN 978-1-4473-5593-9 paperback
ISBN 978-1-4473-5595-3 ePub
ISBN 978-1-4473-5594-6 ePdf

Cover design: Robin Hawes
Front cover image: iStock/marchmeena29
Printed and bound in Great Britain by CMP, Poole
Bristol University Press and Policy Press use environmentally
responsible print partners.

To David

Contents

Acknowledgements

I have acquired a variety of debts during the writing of this book. I would like to offer a number of thanks, both professional and personal.

I am very grateful to the editorial team at Policy Press. Particular thanks should go to my editor, Laura Vickers-Rendell, for her help and support for my proposal. Laura was crucial in shepherding the book from proposal to final manuscript. I also benefited from excellent editorial support from Amelia Watts-Jones, Millie Prekop and Jessica Miles. I am also grateful to Dawn Preston at Newgen Publishing and Alan Halfpenny for their excellence during the production of this book.

I would like to thank the four referees who reviewed the original proposal, as well as the report I received once I submitted my final manuscript. The comments I received were very helpful and certainly improved both the form and content of this book. I hope I have addressed their feedback but any remaining errors are mine alone.

The economics discipline at the Open University was a hospitable environment when I was writing this book, and I have learnt much from colleagues, as well as students.

I would also like to acknowledge that I was able to use some material that I have previously had published elsewhere. I am grateful that I was able to use extracts (or revise) material from the following sources: Prabhakar, R. (2013) 'Asset-based welfare: financialisation or financial inclusion?', *Critical Social Policy*, 33(4): 658–78; Prabhakar, R. (2016) 'How did the Welsh government manage to reform Council Tax in 2005?', *Public Money and Management*, 36(6): 417–24; Prabhakar, R. (2017) 'Why do people opt-out or not opt-out of automatic enrolment? A focus group study of automatic enrolment into a workplace pension in the UK', *Journal of European Social Policy*, 12(5): 447–557; Prabhakar, R. (2018) 'Are basic income versus basic capital debates too narrow?', *Basic Income Studies*, 13(1): 1–6; Prabhakar, R. (2019) 'Financial inclusion: a tale of two literatures', *Social Policy & Society*, 18(1): 37–50; Prabhakar, R. (2019) 'A house divided: asset-based welfare and housing asset-based welfare', *International Journal of Housing Policy*, 19(2): 213–31; Prabhakar, R. (2019) 'Should basic payment accounts be extended?', *Journal of Poverty and Social Justice*, 27(1): 139–44; Prabhakar, R. (2018) 'Millennial bugs. A review of the Resolution Foundation's Intergenerational Commission final report', *The Political Quarterly*, 89(4): 709–13; Prabhakar, R. (2020) 'Universal basic income and Covid-19', *IPPR Progressive Review*, 27(1): 106–13.

My final thanks are to my family and friends. I would like to thank my mother, father, Sajiv, Sadhana, Helen, Maya, Arun, Sheila and Tony for their support during the writing of this book.

Finally, I would like to dedicate this book to my oldest friend David Richardson. We grew up a few doors away from each other in Bradford and have been firm friends ever since. He works for Bradford Council as a financial assessment and welfare benefits officer. He has practical experience of many of the issues covered in this book. It is fitting, then, that the dedication is to him and the work that he does.

Preface

This book is about 'financial inclusion'. Roughly speaking, this refers to policies that seek to encourage individual participation in the financial system. This policy agenda has sparked strong criticisms. A key worry is that financial inclusion ultimately involves shifting people from the security provided by the welfare state and exposing them to the risks and insecurity associated with financial markets.

The aim of this book is to outline and respond to these criticisms. Some of these criticisms are powerful and highlight important shortcomings with financial inclusion. However, one of the key aims of this book is to claim that the financial inclusion agenda should not be rejected in its entirety. The book claims that there is not a single version of financial inclusion and it is possible to shape financial inclusion in different ways. The book suggests that it is important for supporters of financial inclusion to engage with the criticisms but then develop different models of financial inclusion. Inevitably, this will mean further exploration of financial inclusion as different models of financial inclusion may emerge and be examined. The main point is to try and design different approaches rather than giving up on financial inclusion altogether.

This book uses 'financialisation' as a thread to connect different criticisms of financial inclusion. Financialisation is itself the subject of an ever-expanding literature and has many different facets. The most relevant part of the financialisation literature for financial inclusion is the claim that the effort by governments and other organisations to encourage greater participation in the financial system is part of a wider effort to turn people from citizens into investor-subjects. The investor-subject is supposed to make financial investments to secure their own future. A key problem, then, is that investor-subjects are exposed to the risks associated with financial markets and that this ultimately harms individual welfare.

The book looks at what this investor-subject critique means in areas such as saving. One of the points made by the book is that it is important not to see the financial system as separate from the wider economy and so the book looks at the case of housing. The global financial crisis of 2007–08 highlights the way that the financial system and housing are intertwined.

If financialisation structures the criticisms of financial inclusion considered in this book, the main case for the defence of financial inclusion considered here is the idea that it is possible to shape financial inclusion in other directions. To provide evidence of this, the book looks at specific examples where different governments have sought to develop different agendas on financial inclusion. Of course, some of the alternative paths have also attracted criticisms and may not fully convince sceptics. Nevertheless, the reality of different paths highlights that financial inclusion may be developed in different ways.

This book was completed during the COVID-19 pandemic. This pandemic began in late 2019 and spread in 2020. To stop hospitals being overwhelmed by a mass of patients struck down by COVID-19, governments across the world imposed a dizzying set of emergency policies to reduce the transmission of the virus that were not usually seen in peacetime. These included: the closure of schools; the closing down of all 'non-essential' businesses, such as restaurants, bars and cafes; and important restrictions on the freedom of movement and association. Measures such as these appeared (though in different ways) in countries such as China, South Korea, India, Italy, the UK, Spain, Ireland and the US. For example, in March 2020, throughout the UK, citizens were ordered to as far as possible stay at or work from home for a given period, and were only supposed to leave home for a number of restricted purposes, such as buying food, travelling to essential work, taking daily exercise or attending medical appointments.

The COVID-19 crisis prompted mass state intervention in the economy. In the UK, a Conservative government announced in March 2020 a range of support for businesses affected by COVID-19 that amounted to £330 billion, or around 15 per cent of gross domestic product. In March 2020, President Donald Trump signed a Coronavirus Aid, Relief and Economic Act that promised US$2 trillion of federal aid to households and businesses. Among the measures enacted was a set of direct payments to households that amounted to US$1,200 per person for one year and US$500 for each child under 16 years of age. The payments are tapered off for those on high incomes (Edna et al, 2020; HM Treasury, 2020).

One thing laid bare by the pandemic is what services are deemed to be essential in a modern economy. The UK government published a list of key workers who were allowed to travel to their normal place of work during the crisis. These included those working in: health services (such as doctors, nurses or support staff); transport (such as bus drivers); food supply (for example, supermarkets or convenience stores); the police; and utilities (such as electricity, gas or water) (Cabinet Office and Department for Education, 2020).

Financial services were highlighted as one of the key sectors of the economy (Cabinet Office and Department for Education, 2020).

Banking is important as a channel for loans to companies, as well as payments to individuals. For instance, US federal government direct payments to individuals will be made into bank accounts or through cheques. Similarly, payment systems also enabled retailers to encourage payments through contactless cards in order to protect employees through physical distancing. Savings were important for helping people cope with drops in income during the crisis.

An obvious parallel to the COVID-19 pandemic crisis might seem to be the global financial crisis of 2007–08. Both crises involved mass state intervention in the economy and a sense of emergency. However, there are important differences between these two events. Government spending during the COVID-19 crisis might be described as relief as the aim is to protect people and businesses from the economic fallout from the crisis, whereas government spending during the global financial crisis was more geared towards stimulus to pump-prime economic activity.

The COVID-19 emergency underlined the importance of financial services. It creates an opportunity to look at financial inclusion afresh and consider different ways that financial inclusion might be shaped in the future. For example, the emergency direct payments to US citizens might presage innovations in financial inclusion. This book is a contribution to the task of looking at the underpinnings of financial inclusion and the different ways it might be shaped.

1

What is financial inclusion?

Introduction

Financial inclusion has emerged as an important social policy agenda over the past 20 years (Collard, 2007; Mitton, 2008; Marron, 2013; World Bank, 2014; Berry, 2015; Financial Inclusion Commission, 2015; Welsh Government, 2016). Financial inclusion refers broadly to the access that people or groups have to the financial system. The financial system covers areas such as banking, credit, insurance and savings (Berry, 2015; Appleyard et al, 2016; Salignac et al, 2016). Financial exclusion refers to the idea that certain people or groups are denied access to the financial system, and the attention then tends to be on widening participation. Vulnerable groups such as those on low incomes, lone parents or minority ethnic communities may have been excluded from mainstream financial services.

A literature has emerged that is very critical of financial inclusion and sees this as part of the 'financialisation of everyday life' (for a sample of this literature, see Leyshon et al, 2004; Langley, 2008; Montgomerie, 2008; Froud et al, 2010; French et al, 2011; Marron, 2013, 2014; Berry, 2015). The critical literature refers mainly to research published in academic journals or books. As Berry (2015: 510) writes: 'Financial inclusion has invariably been presented as a progressive "response" to financialisation, yet by increasing participation in the financial system, and subjecting greater numbers of people to risks associated with engaging with the financial system, financial inclusion also serves to advance the process of financialisation.' As Berry (2015) notes, financial inclusion is usually presented by government as an avowedly progressive agenda, in that it aims to reduce the inequalities that vulnerable groups, such as single parents or those on low incomes, face in participating in the financial system. Despite this progressive intent, critics claim that financial inclusion ultimately exposes people to the risks associated with the financial system. Critics also see financial inclusion as part of a wider regressive policy of shrinking the welfare state to meet austerity and ideological goals after the 2007–08 global financial crisis.

The supportive literature comes mainly from the policy sector, such as think tanks, politicians, government departments or policy commissions, and is published within policy reports, pamphlets or think pieces (for a sample, see HM Treasury, 1999, 2004, 2007, 2013; Financial Inclusion Taskforce, 2010, 2011a, 2011b; Financial Inclusion Commission, 2015; House of Lords Select Committee on Financial Exclusion, 2017). The applied or supportive literature is much more positive towards financial inclusion. For example, both the Financial Inclusion Commission (2015) and the report of the House of Lords Select Committee on Financial Exclusion (2017) insist on the importance of putting financial inclusion at the heart of government policy.

The critical and supportive literatures are largely developing in parallel and tend not to refer to one another. For example, the House of Lords Select Committee on Financial Exclusion's (2017) final report is supposed to provide a state-of-the-art review of financial exclusion policy. However, the report does not refer at all to critical scholars such as Marron (2013, 2014) or Berry (2015), or to concepts such as financialisation or neoliberalism. Of course, there are notable exceptions to this general pattern. For example, academics such as Rowlingson (Rowlingson and McKay, 2013, 2014, 2015, 2016; Appleyard et al, 2016) and Hills (Hills, 2012; Hills et al, 2013) contribute to both the critical and supportive literatures on financial inclusion. Nevertheless, these figures are exceptions to the overall picture and there is a large gap between the critical and policy work on financial inclusion.

This chapter suggests that it would be much better if there were greater mixing between these different literatures. The critical literature can inform applied work by addressing the issue of which policy avenues are worthy of further development. Conversely, the supportive literature can help develop more nuanced versions of the theoretical literature. Although some strands of financial inclusion policy are likely to contribute to financialisation, other parts of financial inclusion are more likely to reduce the costs faced by vulnerable groups from being excluded from mainstream financial services. Engaging with the supportive literature can help refine the theoretical literature.

Background

The United Kingdom (UK) is a leader in financial inclusion policy and so this book pays particular attention to UK debates. Financial inclusion has its immediate roots in a set of debates during the 1990s. Originally, the focus of these debates was on describing and combating 'financial exclusion'. Much of the interest in financial inclusion was sparked by academic research in geography. This research paid attention to the ways that people or groups faced difficulties in accessing banking. For example, one seam of work looked at the greater challenges that people who live in low-income neighbourhoods have in accessing a physical bank branch (Leyshon and Thrift, 1994, 1995; Kempson and Whyley, 1999).

The Labour governments from 1997 onwards pioneered financial inclusion at a policy level. The Blair government that was elected in 1997 applied the term 'financial exclusion' beyond physical bank branches and towards other financial services. In particular, the Labour government believed that there was a wider range of ways besides material inequality that people might be excluded from opportunity within society (Blair, 1998; Giddens, 1998). Social exclusion was used to capture the idea that exclusion went beyond material inequality. Research suggests that financial exclusion is linked with other health and social outcomes. For example, financial exclusion is associated with the likelihood that people suffer from poorer mental health or may be underweight (Anderloni et al, 2008; Dobbie and Gillespie, 2010; Muir et al, 2015). Policy action teams (PATs) were set up to explore different facets of social exclusion. PAT number 14 was charged with examining exclusion from financial services and published 'Accessing financial services' in 1999 (HM Treasury, 1999).

In the foreword to 'Assessing financial services', Economic Secretary to the Treasury Melanie Johnson says that 'Financial exclusion means that many in those communities, often those in greatest need, do not have the access to financial services the rest of us enjoy, and are worse off as a result' (HM Treasury, 1999: 4). Here, exclusion is understood to refer to the lack of access that people may have to financial services. Similarly, HM Treasury published a strategy document in 2004 called 'Promoting financial inclusion', which states that:

> The term 'financial exclusion' is used in different ways. It can be a broad concept related to a lack of access to a range of financial services or a narrow concept reflecting particular circumstances such as: geographical exclusion; exclusion on the grounds that charges and prices are prohibitively high; or exclusion from marketing efforts. (HM Treasury, 2004: 2)

This statement notes that although financial exclusion may be understood in different ways, a common theme concerns the lack of access that people have to financial services. The Labour government also set up the Financial Inclusion Taskforce to guide policy across government. The Financial Inclusion Taskforce was established in

2005 and had members drawn from across the policy sector (Financial Inclusion Taskforce, 2011; HM Treasury, 2013).

Financial inclusion seemed to drop off the radar after Labour lost the general election in 2010. The Conservative–Liberal Democrat Coalition government formed in 2010 did not renew the Financial Inclusion Taskforce after its term expired in 2011. Explicit references to financial inclusion began to feature less in policy debates. Rowlingson and McKay (2016: 4) comment that: 'The term "financial inclusion" was rarely used by the Coalition government from 2010–2015 even though many policies had an impact on levels of inclusion. ... The new Conservative government also rarely uses the word "financial inclusion" but a number of their policies impact on the nature and level of inclusion.'

As Rowlingson and MacKay (2016) note, although the term 'financial inclusion' dropped out of debates for a period, there were still policies that had a direct impact upon inclusion. Specific policies such as Help to Save as well as the automatic enrolment (AE) of savings into a workplace pension were introduced, and these impinge directly upon financial inclusion and savings. These policies will be examined more closely in Chapter 3.

Efforts have also been made to reintroduce the term 'financial inclusion' into public debates. A Financial Inclusion Commission was set up with the aim of putting 'financial inclusion back on the political agenda ahead of the 2015 General Election' (Financial Inclusion Commission, 2015: 1). The Financial Inclusion Commission was funded by the payments provider MasterCard and had commissioners drawn from the policy sector, including charities, academia and financial services.

The Financial Inclusion Commission (2015) highlights six challenges for the future. First, it calls for leadership in developing a national financial inclusion strategy. It recommends establishing a Minister for Financial Health and the setting up of an expert group to advise this minister. Second, it recommends that banking and payment services meet the needs of low-income consumers. Third, it proposes more affordable credit for those on low incomes and for better debt advice. It notes that credit scores are a key barrier for accessing credit services as those people with either no or a small credit history are often excluded from services or can only access the most expensive services. Fourth, it asks for reforms to support financial resilience and supports policies such as AE into a workplace pension. Fifth, it calls for more affordable provision of insurance. Sixth, there is a focus on financial capability, with recommendations including more education and training from primary school to retirement.

Financial Inclusion Policy Forum

The Financial Inclusion Commission (2015) arguably had several impacts on public policy. It provided a spur, perhaps, for the ad hoc House of Lords Select Committee on Financial Exclusion that was set up in 2016 and reported in 2017. Several members of the Financial Inclusion Commission (2015) were also involved in the government's Financial Inclusion Policy Forum.

As well as a continuity of personnel, various policy ideas floated by the Financial Inclusion Commission (2015) were later enacted by the UK government. In June 2017, the UK government created the post of Parliamentary Under Secretary of State for Pensions and Financial Inclusion (Gov.UK, 2017). In November 2017, the Conservative government also set up a Financial Inclusion Policy Forum, which meets twice a year (HM Treasury, 2018a, 2018b, 2018c). This group is chaired by the Economic Secretary to the Treasury and Minister for Pensions and Financial Inclusion, and includes members drawn from charities, banks, industry bodies and the Financial Conduct Authority. Several commissioners from the Financial Inclusion Commission (2015) are also members of the Financial Inclusion Policy Forum, including Chair of the Financial Inclusion Commission (2015) Sir Sherard Cowper-Coles, Sharon Collard and Sian Williams (HM Treasury and Glen, 2018).

One area where the Financial Inclusion Policy Forum has arguably had an impact is on affordable credit. In the second meeting of the Forum in October 2018, Sian Williams from Toynbee Hall and Eric Leenders from UK Finance led a discussion on this on behalf of the Forum's affordable credit subgroup. The things discussed included reducing the regulatory barriers to affordable credit, increasing investment to social lenders and introducing no-interest loan schemes (HM Treasury, 2018b). The 2018 Budget referred directly to this work on affordable credit: 'Following the work of the Financial Inclusion Policy Forum, the Budget announces new policies to help households manage unexpected costs by increasing access to fair and affordable credit, as well as a consultation scheme for people who fall into problem debt' (HM Treasury, 2018c: 80). The measures announced included a pilot of a no-interest loan scheme, the setting up of an independent body that would manage the £55 million in dormant accounts to support affordable credit and a pilot of prized linked savings schemes for credit unions.

Lack of dialogue between the literatures

A surprising feature of the supportive literature is that it makes very little reference to this critical literature. The Financial Inclusion Commission provides a typical example of this neglect of criticisms. Although the Financial Inclusion Commission provides a state-of-the-art review, it does not refer at all to debates about financialisation or neoliberalism. The supportive literature might not discuss theoretical controversies because it implicitly assumes that financial inclusion is a good thing. Alternatively, the supportive literature might be taking a pragmatic view that financial inclusion is necessary for curbing the excesses of the present economic system. In either case, it would still be beneficial for the supportive literature to engage with critical work. This would allow the supportive literature to improve the content and direction of policy. For example, one danger with a pragmatic turn is that this may breed a fatalistic view that policymakers should be confined to only improving the details of existing (and possibly flawed) policies rather than trying to seek alternatives or different policies. Critical research can help policy work sift through different policies and highlight whether there are specific areas that ought to be developed further and others that ought to be challenged. Reflecting upon theoretical controversies might also build wider support for particular policies because this would directly address the arguments of the critics of those policies.

For example, the supportive literature might draw on critical work on a 'great risk shift' embedded within pension reforms. Rises in the state pension funded through collective taxation is an alternative to encouraging people to save more within defined contribution pension schemes. The state pension shares the risks of retirement throughout society and may be better placed than private schemes to guarantee financial security in retirement.

The recent supportive literature considers pension reforms but devotes most of its energies to those policies that encourage private saving (Financial Inclusion Commission, 2015; House of Lords Select Committee on Financial Exclusion, 2017). For example, the Financial Inclusion Commission (2015) considers initiatives such as AE into a workplace pension and new pension freedoms that focus on the decumulation of defined contribution pension pots. Similarly, the House of Lords Select Committee on Financial Exclusion (2017) calls for an extension of AE to other savings products. Neither report discusses rises in the state pension as an alternative to more private saving for retirement. This limits the policy options on offer. Engaging with critical work would allow the supportive literature to develop a richer range of policy ideas.

Even if the supportive literature confines its attention to reforms such as AE, it would still benefit from engaging with critical work. Scholars have pointed out that there is an important gender inequality embedded within AE (Ginn and MacIntyre, 2013; Grady, 2015; Foster, 2017). Women face a gender pay gap as they have less income than men because they are more likely to have to undertake part-time work to fulfil unpaid caring responsibilities (this is explored further in Chapter 3). This means that women are more likely than men to then fall below the lower earnings threshold for AE. Neither the Financial Inclusion Commission (2015) nor the House of Lords Select Committee on Financial Exclusion (2017) discusses gender and AE. These recent reports would have benefited from engaging with this work on gender when making their recommendations on AE.

Conversely, the theoretical literature would benefit from engaging with the supportive literature and its discussion of different policy choices. The supportive literature highlights the sheer variety of financial inclusion policies and the ways in which they might be designed in different ways. Engaging with the supportive literature would allow critical work to refine its theoretical approaches and develop a more nuanced analysis of financial inclusion.

For example, the critical literature shows how financial capability can be used to deepen neoliberalism. Financial capability concerns the knowledge, skills and confidence of people to make financial decisions. Governments seek to boost financial capability through policies such as financial education. Academic critics suggest that the aim of financial capability is to turn people into consumers for financial markets. Marron (2014: 497) writes that people's:

> failure to live up to the demands of the financialized modern world means their money management, ways of choosing and their motivations must be fundamentally systematized and realigned by authorities. Through an array of programmatic interventions constituting financial capability, this has involved an attempt to bring into reality the figure of the rational, intertemporal consumer.

In the UK, the Financial Services Authority developed the original national strategy for financial capability. Important parts of the Financial

Services Authority's (2006) initial financial capability strategy were arguably used to support neoliberalism. Choosing products, keeping track of finances and staying informed all seem important for creating informed consumers within markets. However, the supportive literature is valuable because it highlights that financial capability can be designed in different ways. Financial capability is evolving in the UK. Much greater emphasis is now placed on using financial capability to support financial resilience. A revised national financial capability strategy says that:

> As people move through their working lives they need to be able to build resilience to cope with financial shocks, such as redundancy, divorce, serious ill health or bereavement, and to plan ahead for life events such as buying a home, starting a family and retirement. People need to be able to budget, create a savings buffer and understand how to avoid financial difficulties. (Money Advice Service, 2015a: 9)

The financial capability strategy has been revised to concentrate on several main themes: managing money well day to day; preparing for life events; and dealing with financial difficulties (Money Advice Service, 2015a, 2015b). This version of financial capability is now much less about helping people become informed consumers and than about supporting them to cope with financial distress, a response in part perhaps to post-2007 austerity measures that have reduced the availability of welfare state safety nets. Engaging with the supportive literature would allow the theoretical literature to acknowledge that financial capability policies do not always have to lead to an investor-subject approach and enable it to fashion a more nuanced analysis of the financialisation of the everyday.

What does financial inclusion mean?

Financial inclusion is used most commonly to refer to the access that people have to mainstream financial services (Financial Inclusion Commission, 2015; House of Lords Select Committee on Financial Exclusion, 2017; HM Treasury and Department for Work and Pensions, 2019). For example, a UK government financial inclusion report for 2018–19 states that '"Financial inclusion" means that individuals, regardless of their background or income, have access to useful and affordable financial products and services. These include products and services such as banking, credit, insurance, pensions and savings, as well as transactions and payment systems, and the use of financial technology' (HM Treasury and Department for Work and Pensions, 2019: 7). Salignac, Muir and Wong (2016) argue that this 'access-point' definition gives rise to a supply-and-demand conception of financial inclusion. Demand-side factors focus on the individual factors that shape access to the financial system. For example, people might lack the knowledge or skills to make decisions in financial markets. Supply-side factors focus on the ways that social policy, regulation and the actions of financial institutions may allow or block access to the financial system. For example, banks might create a barrier for low-income people to open accounts by being unwelcoming to these people.

The specific content of financial inclusion policies might depend on the particular causes of financial exclusion. For example, regulation of financial institutions may be the most appropriate response if supply-side factors are the main reason for financial exclusion. Government intervention or regulation might force financial institutions to lower the barriers they place on certain groups accessing financial services.

Salignac, Muir and Wong (2016) argue that the access-point definition leads to a narrow view of financial inclusion. They say that it is important to recognise that people draw on different resources in their dealings with the financial system. For example, Leyshon and others have developed a 'financial ecologies' approach that highlights how different parts of the population have access to different networks and resources in their engagement with financial markets (Leyshon et al, 2004; French et al, 2011; Salignac et al, 2016). Leyshon et al (2004) distinguish between affluent middle-class consumers and low-income groups in their study of access to retail credit and insurance services. These researchers say that these groups live in rival financial ecologies, with middle-class networks having good access to mainstream financial services and vulnerable groups having a 'relic' ecology dominated by doorstep traders.

Why is financial inclusion important?

Reducing the poverty premium is a key part of the case for reducing financial exclusion: 'exclusion from the financial mainstream often means that consumers pay a "poverty premium" for products and services and have less choice. It can impact their ability to find a job, maintain secure housing, stay physically and mentally healthy and be resilient to changes in income and expenditure' (Financial Inclusion Commission, 2015: 9). The poverty premium refers to the idea that poorer people are more likely than others to suffer exclusion from mainstream financial services. Those who experience exclusion then face extra costs or a premium compared to their peers who can freely access mainstream services. For example, lack of a bank account may contribute to fuel poverty because those on lower incomes cannot take advantage of the cheaper deals on fuel bills available to those who can pay by direct debit (Caplovitz, 1963; Hills, 2012; Financial Inclusion Commission, 2015). There are a variety of estimates of the size of the poverty premium (Westlake, 2011; Davies et al, 2016; Corfe and Keohane, 2018). For example, Davies, Finney and Hartfree (2016) suggest that the poverty premium is £490 per household per year.

Similarly, Lister and Sodha (2006) argue that there is a vulnerability context of poverty which means that people can easily tip into poverty. People may find it difficult to cope with a relatively modest and common shock, such as a washing machine breaking down. People may have to turn to payday lenders to help cope with this shock. Mainstream lenders may not target poorer people because they are unlikely to be a source of profit for these companies (Leyshon et al, 2004). Those denied access to mainstream credit services might then fall prey to payday or fringe lenders that charge very high rates of interest (Appleyard et al, 2016). The Competition and Markets Authority (2015) states that there were 1.8 million payday loan consumers in 2012 and the total loans made were worth £2.8 billion.

The vulnerability context of poverty might also be linked to a related idea of financial resilience. Financial resilience refers broadly to the capacity of people or households to maintain standards of living when faced with adverse events. Salignac et al (2016: 282) argue that financial resilience means asking:

> What appropriate, affordable and accessible resources and supports do people have to draw on at times of financial adversity? Do they have the internal and external resources to assist them to cope in adverse financial circumstances. Reliance enables an asset-based approach and recognises that situations and an individual's ability to cope can shift and change over time and rely on the context, structures and supports that surround them.

Dagdeviren et al (2016) say that the concept of resilience has been applied to people or households facing economic hardship in two main ways. The first application regards the attitudes and skills shown by people or households facing adversity. Dagdeviren et al (2016: 4) say that, 'Regarding the financial crisis and the ensuing recession, this would be the ability, skill and attitude of households to deal with financial shortfalls, increased cost of living, higher debt, and so on, within a particular system.' The second application of the concept of resilience regards the strategies and practices that people and households deploy to cope with adversity.

Strong criticisms of financial resilience have been expressed (Dagdeviren et al, 2016; Hickman, 2018; Donoghue and Edmiston, 2020). Donoghue and Edmiston (2020) present resilience as part of a neoliberal agenda that tends to blame the victim. Here, the emphasis is on active citizenship as a way of getting people to cope with adversity rather than tackling the sources of adversity. They write that, 'Contrary to its claim to empowerment, low-income citizens are being further responsibilised by the resilience agenda and *disempowered* by the social security system upon which they, to varying degrees, rely' (Donoghue and Edmiston, 2020: 24, emphasis in original). Hickman (2018) argues that it is unclear whether resilience is an individual attribute or a process that people or households undergo. He also questions whether or not resilience has positive connotations. Drawing upon a qualitative study of low-income households in Northern Ireland, he claims that resilience is a flawed concept, arguing that the 'suggestion that resilience is in any way a positive phenomenon presents an unrealistic picture of the lives of low-income households struggling with the day-to-day grind of simply coping financially' (Hickman, 2018: 421).

A common theme throughout these criticisms is that the concept of financial resilience ignores the importance of structure or social context. Dagdeviren et al (2016) argue that it is important to instead embed resilience within a social setting. They say that if resilience is isolated from the social context, then the concept would be liable to being misapplied, would have problems in explaining changes in resilience and could be exploited to serve ideological purposes. One response to these points is to reject the concept of financial resilience entirely. A danger with this response is that this may overlook that making decisions about money is likely to be an abiding part of daily life and that the capacity to be able to adapt to shocks is likely to be important for helping people to cope with adversity. A different response, then, may be to accept the importance of such skills but try to embed this in a wider social context that might include other reforms (such as increased benefit levels).

Individual freedom

Supporters of financial inclusion also claim that this agenda is important for individual freedom (Johnson and Sherraden, 2007; McQuaid and Edgell, 2010; Klapper and Singer, 2014; Demirgüç-Kunt et al, 2018). Individual freedom is the subject of a vast literature and there are many different notions of freedom. Politicians of all stripes support individual freedom but have very different understandings of what this value implies. Berlin (1958) makes a classic distinction between negative and positive liberty. Negative liberty refers broadly to a person's 'freedom from' constraint. Governments or other agencies might constrain the choices that a person makes and so negative liberty tries to protect a person's freedom of choice. However, a person might have free choice but this freedom may be purely formal or hollow because they lack the resources to make their choices a reality. Positive freedom embraces an idea of 'freedom to' achieve or attain their choices.

Berlin's (1958) distinction has sparked a huge literature. Different arguments have been advanced for negative or positive liberty. There are also accounts of individual freedom that seek to blend together negative and positive freedom or develop another model of freedom. For example, scholars have argued that there is a distinct concept of republican liberty rooted in the civic republican thought of writers such as Machiavelli or James Harrington. Republican liberty refers to an idea of freedom as non-domination by others. In particular, if a person is forced to depend on others, then this opens up the possibility that people could be vulnerable to outside exploitation. Republican liberty is seen by some as offering a stronger base for individual freedom and independence (Pettit, 1997; Jayasuriya, 2000; White, 2003).

Neoliberalism usually prioritises freedom over other values. Indeed, neoliberalism embeds liberalism within its name. However, neoliberalism usually favours negative liberty. Contributors to neoliberal thought such as Hayek (2001 [1944]) worry about the impact of state intervention on freedom, believing that it leads to serfdom. Most supporters of financial inclusion tend to favour either positive or republican liberty. Access to the financial system is seen as important for turning a person's choices into reality. For example, people usually need money to be able to take advantage of the opportunities that are formally available to them. People may need access to credit to have the necessary money to realise these opportunities. Chapter 2 looks at some of these ideas when it considers capability theory and citizenship.

The role that financial inclusion plays in supporting freedom might be particularly important for certain parts of the population. For example, feminist economics highlights the inequalities that often exist between men and women within the household. In households of men and women, men may use a dominant financial position to exercise broader control over women. For example, in the UK, women usually do the bulk of unpaid caring duties in the household, such as raising children or caring for elderly relatives. Women may then be financially dependent on men, which can undermine their freedom. For example, republican liberty highlights that financial dependence means that women are vulnerable to exploitation through male control in the household. Supporting the financial independence of women may be a practical way of enhancing female freedom. Currently, there are important gender inequalities within the financial system. For example, Demirgüç-Kunt et al (2018: 4) state that 'Women are overrepresented among the unbanked in economies where only a small share of adults are unbanked, such as China and India, as well as in those where half or more are, such as Bangladesh and Colombia.' Financial inclusion offers a route for this female independence.

Self-exclusion

Individual freedom does not, however, provide unambiguous support for financial inclusion. Freedom might also be used to justify self-exclusion, that is, where a person makes a deliberate and informed choice to exclude themselves from the financial system (Salignac et al, 2016; House of Lords Select Committee on Financial Exclusion, 2017). For example, a person might prefer to save money under their bed than in a bank. Salignac, Muir and Wong (2016) argue that it is important to make a distinction between self-exclusion that is voluntary and exclusion that is forced. They write that if people freely choose to exclude themselves, then this should be respected. They note that people feel forced into excluding themselves because they lack the knowledge, say, to make financial decisions: 'Is a person really financially excluded if they choose not to access/use financial products and services? People's choice and agency should be respected. However ... it is important to determine the extent to which an individual has the agency to make an informed choice' (Salignac et al, 2016: 282).

Salignac et al (2016) say that it may not be easy to decide whether exclusion is voluntary or forced. Therefore, they argue that it is important to ensure that people can freely access the financial system because people may change their minds (if exclusion is voluntary) or circumstances may change (if exclusion is forced). Salignac et al (2016: 282) record that a:

> young person who is still living within the family home may not have access to formal credit and would therefore be defined as 'financially excluded'. They will be at little to no risk if they have the resources and supports they can draw from, such as their parents, if they get into a difficult financial situation. They will be at significant risk, however, if they cannot draw on appropriate, affordable and accessible resources and if they are marginalised in other areas.

This quotation reveals at least two points for the discussion of financial inclusion. First, there are alternatives to financial inclusion for meeting individual needs. In this example, the young person's needs are met by their parents. This refers to transfers that may exist within the home and highlights the importance of alternatives to financial inclusion. Chapter 5 will return to this point when it discusses possible alternatives to financial inclusion as a way of achieving public policy goals. Second, the example nevertheless suggests that access to the financial system is a way of supporting the young person's needs. For example, access to credit may ensure that the young person has enough money to achieve their plans. The presence of the financial system may be particularly important in the case where parental support disappears. Thus, even if family support is an alternative to financial inclusion, access to the financial system may still be important for helping the young person to adapt to changing conditions.

An example: reducing the unbanked

The financial inclusion agenda has been applied to a wide variety of areas. Different areas of financial services include banking, credit, savings and insurance. There is also a large variety within each of these areas. Reducing the 'unbanked' – that is, those people without access to a bank account – is an important example of financial inclusion. Access to a bank account is particularly important as a bank account is usually a gateway to other financial services, such as mainstream credit (Financial Inclusion Commission, 2015; House of Lords Select Committee on Financial Exclusion, 2017; Demirgüç-Kunt et al, 2018). Lack of a bank account imposes various costs on individuals. For example, employers in high-income countries usually prefer paying wages directly into a bank account. Being unbanked creates a barrier for gaining paid employment, and this can then limit individual independence and opportunity. Other cash transfers, such as benefits, may also be made more difficult without access to a bank account.

Demirgüç-Kunt et al (2018) estimate that there are around 1.7 billion adults around the world that are unbanked. These researchers argue that most of the unbanked live in the developing world. They say that about half of the unbanked live in seven countries, namely, Bangladesh, China, India, Indonesia, Mexico, Nigeria and Pakistan. Demirgüç-Kunt et al (2018) state that women form the majority (56 per cent) of the unbanked across the world, and that a lack of money is the most common reason for being unbanked. Demirgüç-Kunt et al (2018: 1) spell out the importance of being banked, and financial inclusion more generally, when they state: 'Financial services can help drive development. They help people to escape poverty by facilitating investments in their health, education and businesses. And they make it easier to manage financial emergencies – such as job loss or crop failure – that can push families into destitution.'

Concern with the unbanked is not confined to the developing world. Basic payment accounts are also an important part of the European Union's policy on banking inclusion (Gómez-Barroso and Marbán-Flores, 2013; European Commission, 2014). The European Union issued a Payment Accounts Directive in 2014 that requires all member states to make available payment accounts with basic features. A payment account is understood to refer to 'an account held in the name of one or more payment service users which is used for the execution of payment transactions' (European Union, 2015a: 23). Across the European Union, basic payment accounts allow people to make deposits, withdraw money and receive and carry out payments such as direct debits. These accounts do not have to offer overdraft or credit facilities (European Union, 2017). The European Union has also issued the Payments Accounts Directive 2, which makes it easier for consumers to share their account details with third parties online. This move towards 'open banking' also makes it easier for third parties to make payments from a bank account as an alternative to credit or debit cards (European Union, 2015b). In the UK, basic bank accounts (BBAs) are the main accounts aimed at the unbanked (HM Treasury, 2015a; House of Lords Select Committee on Financial Exclusion, 2017; Edmonds, 2017). Research from the University of Birmingham suggests that just over a million adults in the UK were unbanked in 2018 (McKay et al, 2019). Reviews have called for BBAs to be extended (Financial Inclusion Commission, 2015; House of Lords Select Committee on Financial Exclusion, 2017).

Research suggests that lack of money is the most common reason for being unbanked (Demirgüç-Kunt et al, 2018). This highlights a point that will be explored in later chapters, namely, that ensuring that people have enough money is likely to be an important part of any adequate reform of financial inclusion. Addressing the lack of money may be one important way of reducing the unbanked. Basic payment accounts might be linked with policies aimed at encouraging saving among low-income individuals. Sherraden (1991) crafted an Individual Development Account (IDA) scheme that allows public or private agencies to match personal savings made into a special account that is dedicated for personal development, such as investing in training, starting a business or putting down a deposit for a home. Trials of matched savings accounts have occurred in places such as Uganda (Karimli et al, 2014).

Governments might also tie basic payment accounts to credit policies that are well suited to those on low incomes. One way of doing this is for governments to support credit unions as a way of providing basic payment accounts. Credit unions are cooperative organisations that usually reduce the barriers that low-income people and households face in accessing credit services. The House of Lords Select Committee on Financial Exclusion (2017: 83) states that 'Credit unions had traditionally obtained their deposits from their members, who were by definition the same, generally low-income customer base as the cohort to whom they would lend.' Credit unions are admittedly small-scale in places such as the UK but linking basic payment accounts to credit unions might be a way of encouraging account holders to use their bank account while also giving them access to a suitable level of credit.

One current challenge is to boost the use of bank accounts. One way of trying to encourage greater use, particularly in the developing world, is to digitise utility payments such as electricity or water. Demirgüç-Kunt et al (2018: 103) say that 'Arguably the single best way to increase account use would be to more fully digitize payments for water, electricity, and other utility bills.' They say that in 2017, 81 per cent of account holders in Egypt paid utility bills in cash, and in both Brazil and Indonesia, around 25 million women with an account used cash to pay utility bills. They also propose that linking mobile phone technology with bank accounts and formalising savings may be practical steps for encouraging greater use of bank accounts. Klapper and Singer (2014) argue that digitising payments can boost female economic empowerment because, unlike cash transfers, digital payments are often private information and thereby give women greater control over money than having to surrender cash to males within the household. Open banking offers the prospect to advance digital payments, though it should also be acknowledged that there are risks associated with cyber-security, such as accounts being hacked and the theft of personal data (Edmonds, 2018).

Financialisation

Financial inclusion is subject to strong criticism as well as support. Research on financialisation is the main source of criticism of financial inclusion (Langley, 2008; Montgomerie, 2008; Froud et al, 2010; Coppack, 2013; Van der Zwan, 2014; Appleyard et al, 2016). Research on financialisation emerged during the 1990s and has grown rapidly since the global financial crisis of 2007–08. Financialisation refers to the spread and increasing importance of financial markets within the economy and society. As Van der Zwan (2014: 99, emphasis in original) writes: 'Since the late 1990s and early 2000s, scholars from a variety of disciplines – including political science, sociology, anthropology, geography and economics – have used the concept of *financialization* to describe this shift from industrial to finance capitalism.'

The literature on financialisation is very varied and contains a number of threads. Van der Zwan (2014) highlights three main strands of financialisation in her overview of this literature. The first is the role that financial markets play in accumulation in modern economies. Theorists of financialisation claim that financial markets have replaced methods such as 'Fordism' for economic growth. Fordism refers to the mass manufacturing of standard products such as cars on mass assembly lines. The second strand of financialisation is the spread of a shareholder model of the firm. This means that the managers of companies seek only to maximise shareholder interests, which usually means profits. The third strand of financialisation is the financialisation of the everyday, which charts the way that financial markets shape the everyday life of people and households.

The financialisation of the everyday is the most relevant strand when thinking about financial inclusion. McIntosh and Wright (2019) argue that the concept of 'lived' experience is becoming more common in social policy research. Although this concept has intuitive appeal, they ask whether it has solid content, writing: 'what is any experience if it is not lived?' (McIntosh and Wright, 2019: 450). They explore the different theoretical strands that feed into this concept and claim that the idea of 'lived' does add something to experience. They argue that lived experience can give an insight into the typical lives shared by many people. This might also highlight the inequalities faced by specific groups in society, such as women. McIntosh and Wright (2019: 463) state that lived experience can be 'associated with an empathetic immersion in the lives and concerns of people affected by and involved in policy processes and outcomes, including elite policy makers and influential context creators, managers and front-line workers as well as disempowered and oppressed groups'. The concept of lived experience provides a reason for studying the everyday life of finance. Everyday decisions about money are likely to be an important part of the lived reality shared by many people.

Critics worry that financial inclusion may merely expose people to the risks associated with the financial system (Van der Zwan, 2014; Langley, 2008; Finlayson, 2009; Montgomerie and Tepe-Belfrage, 2017; Lai, 2017; Santos, 2017). During the 20th century, the welfare state has arisen as a way of protecting people against the risks they face in everyday life, such as losing their job, becoming sick or falling into poverty upon retirement. Under a welfare state, the risks associated with providing welfare are spread across society. Although boosting participation in the financial system does not come automatically at the expense of the welfare state, critics nonetheless claim that financial inclusion ultimately involves rolling back the welfare state in favour of individual investment within financial markets. Van der Zwan (2014: 113–14) says that the 'expansion of financial markets has coincided with the retreat of the welfare state in many of the advanced political economies, but particularly in the USA and UK'.

Individual investment products linked to market performance expose individuals to significant risks. For example, a state pension might provide financial security in retirement. An alternative to this is to encourage private saving into a defined contribution scheme. However, people are then exposed to a risk that their pension investments may perform poorly (Hacker, 2008; Standing, 2011). People are exposed not only to poor investment performance, but also to high charges that significantly impact the size of entitlements, particularly when returns are poor. Standing (2011) argues that financial institutions were mainly responsible for the global financial crisis of 2007–08 and that this had a direct effect on pensioners because it depleted the size of final pension pots after the crisis. He writes that 'Savers have done nothing wrong, except to follow the urgings of successive governments over two decades. The International Monetary Fund, World Bank and Organisation for Economic Co-operation and Development (OECD) had all eulogised "private savings accounts" and defined contribution private pensions. Now those who took their advice were penalised' (Standing, 2011: 13).

People might also be exposed to more systemic risks within the banking system. Mis-selling scandals occur when financial institutions provide misleading information on goods or services, such as hidden payment protection insurance charges on loans in the UK. In the United States (US), a 'sub-prime mortgage' crisis involved banks and other financial institutions encouraging low-income individuals and households to overextend themselves and take unsustainable levels of personal debt. Problems in this sub-prime mortgage market were one of the triggers for the global financial crisis of 2007–08 (Ferran, 2012; Garratt et al, 2014; Sane and Halan, 2017; Kotarski and Brkic, 2017).

Subjects or agents?

Many of these critics treat financial inclusion as a cultural project to turn people into subjects. Rowlingson, Appleyard and Gardner (2016: 530) note that this ' "financialisation of everyday life" approach sees citizens being transformed from "welfare subjects" to "personal investors" and "personal borrowers" with a related internalisation of new norms of individual risk-taking'.

Much of this work draws upon ideas within sociology, especially Foucault's notion of governmentality (Langley, 2008; Finlayson, 2009; Van der Zwan, 2014; Montgomerie and Tepe-Belfrage, 2017; Lai, 2017; Santos, 2017). Lai (2017: 916) argues that the 'Foucauldian notion of governmentality has been particularly influential in financialisation studies regarding how states regulate behaviour "at a distance" through discourses of "personal responsibility" and "self-sufficiency"'. For Foucault (2007), the individual is subject to general forces that control their life. The state has developed various means that allow it to observe and control each person. When applied to financial inclusion, this means that the government uses this agenda to mould people into accepting the demands of financial markets.

The stress placed upon subjection may be seen above all in the figure of the 'investor-subject' that stalks this literature (Langley, 2008; Finlayson, 2009; Montgomerie and Tepe-Belfrage, 2017; Lai, 2017; Santos, 2017). An investor-subject is required to make investments for their own welfare. In making these investments, people are thereby subject to the risks associated with financial markets, namely, that people may make poor investment choices or that any investments they do make perform poorly because of factors beyond their control. People might also be subject to systemic risks, such as bank mis-selling scandals.

The figure of the investor-subject is cast in abstract terms. However, the term is elastic enough to be able to be applied to different parts of the population. Perhaps most obviously, this may be thought to apply to adults of working age. These individuals might invest in a range of financial products, such as shares, bonds or savings, or perhaps non-financial investments such as housing, though people may have to borrow on mortgage markets to buy a home, thereby making a link between financial markets and housing.

The investor-subject approach may also be relevant outside this core group of subjects. It might also apply to those parts of the population that are not usually associated with investment. For example, school-age children may not usually be required to make investments in financial products. Nevertheless, the investor-subject approach may be relevant in other ways. For example, policy might encourage financial education in schools. The content of the financial education might be aimed at teaching children the basics of investment, thereby preparing them to be fully fledged investor-subjects in adult life. Similarly, those people who are retired may not now be saving into a pension. The retired might have to make choices over how to use their defined contribution pension pots. Some of these choices may involve further investments, such as whether or not to buy an annuity. This means that there are likely to be a variety of experiences associated with an investor-subject and so there are different types of investor-subjects.

Financialisation and neoliberalism

Research on financialisation has its roots in political economy. In particular, the spread of financial markets has been linked to a neoliberal or free market agenda. This association with neoliberalism highlights an ideological side to financial inclusion, namely, that particular policy choices may reflect, at least in part, ideological or political choices. Although financialisation and neoliberalism have been closely linked, they are nevertheless distinct (Davis and Walsh, 2017; Karwowski, 2019). As Davis and Walsh (2017: 31) write: 'When considering how they each manifest in the real world, financialization and neoliberalism are clearly related but different. The ways and degrees to which neoliberal economies have become financialized have varied considerably, as some states have much larger financial centres, relative to their industry and state sectors, than others.'

The ideological side to financialisation perhaps leads to a critique of financial inclusion. Critics of financial exclusion may contend that it is better to chart an alternative to free markets than boosting access to the financial system. In particular, neoliberalism or free markets might be deemed to be the source of a range of exclusions that include but go beyond financial exclusion. Critics might accept that financial inclusion might succeed in reducing a poverty premium but claim that it is more important for policymakers to address the underlying economic system that gives rise to the problems in the first place. This means that even if critics accept the relevance of the poverty premium, they might still insist that financial inclusion distracts from more urgent issues.

Even if advocates accept that a deeper issue is to reform free markets, they may nevertheless say that creating such an alternative is a bigger and more long-lasting task. People and households will still face immediate issues and it is important to tackle these immediate concerns even if more weight is placed on reforming free markets. Reducing the poverty premium and creating an alternative to neoliberalism may not be mutually exclusive.

A different response may go further and disentangle financialisation from neoliberalism. Davis and Walsh (2017) argue that financialisation differs from neoliberalism in five main ways. First, the financial sector is able to create money by developing complex products, whereas neoliberalism focuses more narrowly on the control or allocation of the money supply. Second, the key concern in finance markets is with transactions, whereas neoliberalism has a broader set of concerns over things such as the costs of raw materials or factors of production such as land, labour and capital. Third, financialisation suggests that financial markets are the best way to allocate capital across an economy, whereas neoliberalism allows the possibility that other types of market are the best for allocating resources in an economy. Fourth, financial markets stress the dominant role that shareholders or financial investors should play in the governance of corporations, whereas neoliberalism allows for a greater role for stakeholders in the governance of corporations. Fifth, participants in financial markets concentrate mainly on the microeconomic level, whereas neoliberal policymakers examine both the microeconomic and macroeconomic levels. Davis and Walsh (2017: 32) admit that financialisation and neoliberalism often overlap:

> at a general ideological level, neoliberal economists and financiers agree on a range of economic measures, from low taxes and market deregulation to free trade and free movement of capital. When comparing the core economic principles and intellectual paradigms of the two, both are in favour of markets and advocates of global free trade.

The view that financialisation and neoliberalism are distinct means that it may be possible to decouple financialisation from neoliberalism.

The financialisation of the everyday might also refer to a person's 'lived experience' or 'lived reality' of money (Appleyard et al, 2016; Rowlingson et al, 2016). This recognises that it costs people money to live, for example, people need money to pay the rent or mortgage, buy food, or heat the home. Indeed, the economic reality is that many (and perhaps most) of the people who suffer from financial exclusion are not able to be investors within financial markets. In principle, the financialisation of the everyday that refers to a person's lived experience of money applies to any economic system. People still need money to live on in a system in which finance is largely socialised. This means that the link between financialisation and neoliberalism refers to a specific version of the financialisation of the everyday but that alternatives exist. Rolling back neoliberalism does not necessarily erase the financialisation of the everyday.

Structure of this book

This chapter claims that this split between the critical and supportive literatures impoverishes research on financial inclusion. The supportive literature does not usually discuss theoretical controversies over financial inclusion and instead confines itself to the details of policy. The lack of engagement with theoretical controversies means that the supportive literature does not unpick whether there are specific strands of financial inclusion policy that ought to be developed further and whether there are other types of policy that ought to be challenged more clearly. The critical literature provides a blunt treatment of financial inclusion policy. It does not engage with the discussion of policy choices within the supportive literature and so does not consider that it is possible to design financial inclusion in different ways. Some of the different versions of financial inclusion may address the critical concerns about this agenda. There is also a danger that the academic literature overlooks the fact that the financialisation of the everyday may amount to people's lived experience of money and that it costs money to live on whatever social and economic system is in place.

This chapter therefore claims that it would be much better for research for the different literatures to cross-breed. This cross-fertilisation of ideas can occur across all of the areas of financial inclusion and so can cover banking, savings, insurance and guidance or advice. An inclusive approach is now needed for further progress in research on financial inclusion.

Chapter 2 examines financial capability. The chapter notes that financial inclusion refers broadly to the access that people have to the financial system. However, it is possible that people have full access to the financial system but still make poor choices because they lack the capacity to make informed choices. Conversely, people might be fully capable of making such choices but are unable to make these choices if they are excluded from financial services.

This points to the importance of 'financial capability' as a complement to financial inclusion. Financial capability refers to the knowledge, skills and confidence of people to make financial choices. Critics claim that financial capability ultimately turns people into consumers or 'investor-subjects'. The chapter argues that while it is possible for financial capability to develop in this fashion, it can also be part of an alternative agenda that supports citizenship. The capacity of people to make financial decisions is an important part of citizenship and so the task is to shape financial capability in appropriate ways rather than rejecting the idea outright.

Chapter 3 turns from the theoretical debates covered in the opening chapters and explores policy agendas associated with financial inclusion. There are many possible agendas associated with financial inclusion but the chapter looks at savings as this has been the site of some of the most innovative financial inclusion policies, such as asset-based welfare and the automatic enrolment of people into savings products.

'Asset-based welfare' encourages the individual ownership of assets such as savings, pensions and property. This resulted in policies such as the Child Trust Fund (CTF) and Help to Save in the UK, and the IDA initiative in the US. Bodies such as the House of Lords Select Committee on Financial Exclusion (2017) and the Financial Inclusion Commission (2015) both support the automatic enrolment of people into savings policies. The UK has recently implemented the automatic enrolment into a workplace pension, which is the most important national scheme of its kind anywhere in the world and is attracting international interest.

Critics suggest that these policies are ultimately aimed at turning people into investor-subjects and are used to replace the welfare state. However, the chapter argues that such policies might also be used to tackle poverty and to support citizenship. Much depends on how such policies are designed. The chapter considers different ways of adapting asset-based policies, as well as steps such as 'progressive universalism' within the CTF and the relevance of tackling gender inequality within the automatic enrolment of a workplace pension.

Chapter 4 studies the case of housing. The figure of the 'investor-subject' is key to the critique of financial inclusion policy. This figure highlights the importance of considering the special role of housing for at least two reasons. First, housing is arguably the most important investment that is made by investor-subjects. For example, IDAs are supposed to be used for three main aims, namely, paying for training, starting a business or putting down a deposit on a home. In fact, critics of asset-based welfare claim that this specific policy agenda is focused mainly on boosting home-ownership and so there is now a literature that is dubbed 'housing asset-based welfare'.

Second, investors often have to borrow on mortgage markets to pay for a home. This highlights that 'borrowing to invest' is a key part of an investor-subject approach. Critics say that 'borrowing to invest' led to record levels of personal indebtedness and fuelled a house price bubble that was one of the triggers for the global financial crisis of 2007–08. For critics, this shows that the financial inclusion agenda contributed directly to the instability within the economy.

The chapter argues that many of the supporters of asset-based welfare neglect the role played by housing. It argues that it is important for defenders of financial inclusion to confront these arguments directly. The chapter also argues that financial inclusion need not necessarily lead to a house price bubble and instead might be used to open up debates about the nature of home-ownership.

One of the claims made in this book is that it is possible to disentangle financial inclusion from neoliberalism. Chapter 5 considers some of the possible alternatives for financial inclusion. The aim is to consider the ways in which it might be possible for the everyday life of finance to develop in different directions. The first part of Chapter 5 considers alternative policy ideas, such as a universal basic income as well as universal basic services. The second part of Chapter 5 examines the feasibility of an alternative future. To do this, it studies what lessons might be drawn from the Welsh government reforms of property taxation.

Chapter 6 concludes by considering some of the things that critics of financial inclusion might learn from its supporters. The chapter uses the example of the financial education of young people to highlight the varying nature of policy, which might also inform theoretical discussions of the everyday life of finance. Chapter 6 also suggests some possible further areas of research that build upon some of the arguments contained in this book.

2

Financial capability: citizens or subjects?

Introduction

Chapter 1 suggested that financial inclusion tries to encourage individual participation in the financial system. If people are to take part in the financial system, then they need both access to the financial system and the capacity and motivation to make financial decisions. This chapter considers financial capability. Financial capability refers broadly to the knowledge, skills and confidence of people to make financial decisions.

Financial capability has been a particular area of policy concern since the global financial crisis of 2007–08 (Commission for Financial Capability, 2015; National Strategy for Financial Literacy, 2015; Financial Investor Education Foundation, 2019). One of the main reasons for this is the view that shortfalls in financial capability are thought to have contributed directly to the financial crisis. O'Donnell and Keeney (2010: 362) comment that the global financial crisis 'only serves to highlight the importance of financial capability. It can be argued that the sub-prime crisis in the US which had such global ramifications was a manifestation of poor levels of financial capability there.' For example, people and households were thought to have made poor decisions and housing investments that created the conditions for the financial crisis.

Governments have sought to address these shortfalls in financial capability through policies such as financial education. Critics see the stress on financial education as part of an effort to create investor-subjects. As Santos (2017: 414) writes:

> Financial education policy must be put in the context of contemporary capitalist societies that are engendering a transformation of citizens into consumers where collectively earned individualised rights are being replaced by increased access to a wider panoply of commodified products and services. It must be perceived, in particular, as part of a

broader strategy that aims at promoting the expansion of financial markets at the expense of collective forms of provision, based on intensifying household relations with financial markets as borrowers, investors and insurers.

The attention paid to financial capability might be part of a wider concern with a focus on individual behaviour within welfare policy. This suggests that this is part of a shift in responsibility from the state to individuals. Donoghue and Edmiston (2020: 9) refer to the attention paid to active citizenship as being part of the 'continued reorientation of social citizenship towards neoliberal, productivist ends'. Against this, one might counter that individual behaviour is important for individual well-being. Brüggen et al (2017) propose a concept of financial well-being, which refers to a person's perception of being able to achieve and maintain standards of living. This notion of financial well-being is subjective and concentrates on living standards both now and in the future. They say that this concept puts 'behavior at the heart of the model because it has a direct impact on financial well-being. Possible behaviors include breaking financially destructive behaviors, stimulating sound financial behaviors, or stabilizing behaviors during critical life situations' (Brüggen, 2017: 231).

This chapter defends the concept of financial capability and suggests that it may be moulded in different ways. Although one version might indeed be part of a cultural project to turn people into investor-subjects, other versions might also be used to support social citizenship. Perhaps the most plausible model here is one that overlaps with a capability approach. This chapter claims that there are debates over how best to build financial capability. This touches on recent debates over the merits of financial education versus behavioural nudges. The chapter concludes by suggesting that people need access to money as well as financial capability if their financial well-being is to be enhanced.

What is financial capability?

Researchers have often paid scant attention to financial capability. Lusardi and Mitchell (2011: 498) state that 'relatively few researchers prior to year 2000 incorporated financial literacy into theoretical models of saving and financial decision-making'. 'Financial literacy' was originally the preferred term used within policy debates. This referred broadly to the capacity to understand financial matters. Although the term 'financial literacy' is still used, there has been a growing shift to referring to financial capability. One reason for this is a growing belief among academics and policymakers that there are other things besides knowledge and skills that are important for decision-making. These other things include behavioural dispositions, attitudes and confidence. Atkinson et al (2007: 29) report that 'As such it is far more than basic skills making the term "capability" more appropriate than "literacy".'

UK research on financial capability is influential in the international efforts to harmonise the measurement of financial capability across different countries. For example, researchers at the Personal Finance Research Centre at the University of Bristol helped develop the UK's first national survey of financial capability. These contributions have been influential in international efforts to develop common measures for financial capability in different countries (Atkinson et al, 2007; Kempson, 2009; Atkinson and Messy, 2012). The general importance of UK research into financial capability at an international level provides a rationale for looking more closely at how financial capability is understood in the UK.

Evidence suggests that there are important shortfalls in financial capability across the world (Atkinson et al, 2007; Lusardi and Mitchell, 2011, 2014). In the UK, the Financial Services Authority commissioned the first national survey of financial capability in 2005. The Money Advice Service (2015a, 2015b, 2018) followed this up with surveys in 2015 and 2018. These surveys suggest that levels of financial capability vary across different parts of the population. The Money Advice Service (2015a, 2015b) reports particular issues facing young people and the unemployed. For example, it says that 51 per cent of those aged 18–24 are managing their money well compared with 65 per cent of those aged 55–74. The 2015 survey repeated the questions that were asked a decade earlier. The Money Advice Service (2015a, 2015b) notes that there has been a worsening of financial capability in some areas. For instance, 78 per cent of respondents were able to read a bank balance correctly on a bank statement in 2015, compared with 91 per cent of respondents in 2005.

The OECD (2016, 2018) has been coordinating efforts to measure financial capability across the world (Kempson, 2009; Atkinson and Messy, 2012). It has created an overall index of financial literacy based on scores achieved for financial knowledge, behaviour and attitudes. The OECD (2016) states that overall levels of financial literacy are relatively low. It reports results for 29 countries (both inside and outside the OECD), including Poland, Brazil, the UK, Finland, Jordan and Canada. The average score for all participating countries is 13.2 out of 21. The lowest-scoring country is Poland (11.6) and the highest-scoring country is France (14.9).

The Money Advice Service (2015a, 2015b) is responsible for the national financial capability strategy in the UK. It has created a hub that contains all the current work on financial capability (see: www.fincap. org.uk/uk_strategy). The definition of financial capability has evolved over time. The Financial Services Authority's original definition of financial capability had five main themes (Financial Services Authority, 2003, 2006; Atkinson et al, 2007):

- Staying informed. This facet looks at the extent to which people keep informed about the general economy, such as the inflation rate or interest rates.
- Keeping track of finances. This examines the extent to which people look closely at their personal finances, such as reading bank statements and salary statements, or keeping track of bills.
- Making ends meet. This focuses on whether people are able to manage their household budgets effectively, for example, looking at both income and expenditure.
- Planning ahead. This examines how well people are planning ahead for the future. Here, particular attention is paid to the plans people have in place for retirement.
- Making choices. This aspect studies the extent to which people can make informed choices when they are making consumer purchases.

This understanding of financial capability centres on an individual's knowledge and skills. This definition does not refer to the access that people have to the financial system. However, access to the financial system is important if people are to be able to make financial decisions. A person may possess knowledge and skills but may be stopped from making decisions because of lack of access to the financial system.

Financial capability and financial inclusion

It is important to link financial capability with financial inclusion, that is, access to the financial system. There is growing recognition of the importance of this connection (Atkinson et al, 2007; Johnson and Sherraden, 2007; OECD, 2016). The OECD (2016: 54) states that 'It is globally recognised that financial literacy and financial inclusion, along with a robust consumer protection framework, are vital to the empowerment of individuals and the overall stability of the financial system.'

The main measures that have been developed to assess the extent to which a person is 'connected' to the financial mains are at an early stage.

The OECD (2016) uses four main metrics for financial inclusion. First is the holding of different financial products, such as savings accounts, credit cards, some form of insurance or mobile payment accounts. This assesses the links to savings, credit and insurance markets. Second is the public awareness of different financial products. This awareness is an important prior stage before any connection to the financial system. Third is the choice of different financial products. This explores the extent to which people have exercised a choice over different types of product over the last couple of years. This looks at how far people have monitored, compared and then chosen a product from different options. Fourth is the extent to which people rely on alternatives to the formal financial system, such as relying on informal networks like family or friends.

In the UK, references to financial inclusion have become more important for discussions of financial capability. The Money Advice Service (2015a: 8, emphasis in original) says that financial capability is 'driven by personal skills, knowledge, attitudes and motivations, and made possible by an inclusive financial system and supportive social environment. Financial capability helps people achieve the best possible financial well-being.'

This definition has three main parts. First, there is an emphasis on skills and knowledge. This part of the definition draws upon the five areas outlined in the Financial Services Authority's (2006) definition of financial capability, that is, staying informed, keeping track of finances, making ends meet, planning ahead and making choices.

Second, there is attention to 'mindset'. This refers to general attitudes and motivation, such as the confidence of people to make financial decisions. The attention to mindset recognises that if people are to make financial decisions, then they must be both able *and* willing to make decisions.

Third, the definition mentions an inclusive financial system and supportive social environment. This acknowledges that ease of access to the financial system is important if people are to make financial decisions.

The capability approach

One might argue that financial capability is part of a neoliberal approach to welfare (Donoghue and Edmiston, 2020). One response to the claim that financial capability is turning citizens into consumers is to say that it is possible for people to be both citizens and consumers. People might enjoy the rights and entitlements associated with citizenship while also making choices in markets. Marshall (1950) offers a classic statement of the development of citizenship. He presents citizenship as an accumulation of civil, political and social rights. Marshall argues that: civil rights such as free speech emerged during the 17th century; political rights such as the right to vote had solidified by the 19th century; and the main legacy of the 20th century has been to outline social rights such as health or education.

Marshall's account of citizenship has prompted a number of debates. For example, scholars have questioned whether citizenship evolved in the way that he describes. Marquand (1997) argues that the provision of civil rights in the UK is incomplete and so there has been no steady path from civil, to political, to social rights. Feminist scholarship also casts doubt on the idea that women have always enjoyed the same rights as men. For example, women have often been granted voting rights later than men and this counters the view that political rights were firmly established during the 19th century. Lister (2003 [1997]) claims that it is important to develop gendered notions of citizenship in order to recognise and address the gaps that exist between men and women.

One might also claim that even if financial capability supports people to be consumers, this can coexist alongside the rights of citizens. Opponents might contend that the domain of a consumer expands at the expense of that of a citizen. Governments might erode social rights by replacing previous entitlements with a demand that people should provide for themselves through the market. Although it may be possible to combine being a citizen and consumer in theory, in practice, governments might use the latter to scale back the former.

Supporters of financial capability contend that it strengthens social citizenship. The main way this is done is by claiming that financial capability is part of Amartya Sen's capability approach (Johnson and Sherraden, 2007; McQuaid and Edgell, 2010; Balakrishnan et al, 2011; Storchi and Johnson, 2016). The capability approach covers a wide set of theories and a large literature (Jayasuriya, 2000; Robeyns, 2005, 2016). Robeyns (2016) argues that it is important to distinguish between the capability approach as a general view and specific theories or accounts of capability. Key contributors to the capability approach include scholars such as Amartya Sen and Martha Nussbaum. There are many different capability accounts and theories, and it is hard to summarise these in a simple way (Hick, 2012; Robeyns, 2005, 2016). Robeyns (2016) provides a critical overview that applies a 'cartwheel' to understanding the capability approach. She argues that the centre of the cartwheel is the core of the capability approach, and that capabilities and functionings belong to the core (Robeyns, 2016). Capabilities focus on what a person is able to be or do. Functionings are what a person has achieved, for example, what they have done or the state of being that they have attained. She says that all capability theories 'focus on what a person is able to be and to do (her capabilities) and/or those capabilities that she has realized (her functionings)' (Robeyns, 2016: 403). The rest of the cartwheel is made up of a periphery of different parts. Robeyns (2016) refers to issues such as the purpose of capability theory, measurement and empirical issues, and the selection of functionings and capabilities.

Sen (1985, 1992, 1998, 2009) is usually credited as being the founder of the capability approach. Other scholars have developed capability theory in other directions. For example, Nussbaum (2000, 2011) draws on political theory to outline a distinct version of capability theory rooted in social justice. The bulk of the financial inclusion literature tends to refer to Sen's theory (Johnson and Sherraden, 2007; McQuaid and Edgell, 2010; Balakrishnan et al, 2011; Storchi and Johnson, 2016). The attention given to Sen in the financial inclusion literature provides a case for looking more closely at his ideas.

Sen's theory is set against two important approaches for spreading resources throughout society. The first is a standard economic approach which proposes that resources should be spread to maximise utility: individuals are assumed to have a fixed set of preferences; people derive utility or happiness from satisfying these preferences; and resources should be spread to maximise utility. This approach has its roots in the utilitarian thinking in the 19th century. Sen argues that this view fails to recognise that people may simply adapt their preferences to match their constraints and so individual happiness may be a poor guide to individual welfare.

The second approach is an equal shares view which suggests that resources should be divided equally throughout society. Ronald Dworkin (1981) is most closely linked with this approach. Sen (1985, 1998, 2009) says that a problem with the equal shares view is that it overlooks the fact that certain people in society need a greater share of resources than others to enjoy a similar standard of living. For example, some people with physical disabilities need extra resources so that they can have a similar standard of living compared to others.

Sen's (1985, 1992, 1998, 2009) theory has had an important impact on public policy. For example, his capability theory underpins the United Nations (UN) Human Development Index. The Human Development Index focuses on three core capabilities, namely, the ability to have a healthy life, the ability to acquire knowledge and the ability to attain a decent standard of living. Different means are important for achieving these different capabilities. The UN uses average and expected years of schooling as a way of measuring the ability to acquire knowledge, and gross national income per capita to measure the capacity to achieve a given standard of living (United Nations Development Programme, 2018).

Capability and freedom

Sen makes a direct link between the capability approach and individual freedom. He claims that the 'capability to achieve functionings (i.e. all of the alternative combinations of functionings a person can choose to have) will constitute the person's freedom – the real opportunities – to have well-being' (Sen, 1992: 40). Here, the link between capability and freedom provides a reason for implementing his approach. In particular, pursuing a capability approach is important for supporting individual freedom.

Jayasuriya (2000) suggests that Sen's capability theory implies a republican concept of liberty, and claims that Sen's insight is to realise that positive freedom is needed as a platform for negative freedom: 'In short, real freedom to choose (a form of negative freedom) needs a dose of positive freedom in order to enable individuals to achieve certain kinds of capabilities' (Jayasuriya, 2000: 290). Negative freedoms focus on the freedom of choice and the absence of constraints. Positive freedom concentrates on what a person is able to do. Jayasuriya (2000) argues that this mix of positive and negative liberty yields a view of freedom as non-domination by others.

Robeyns (2016) argues that although there is a link between Sen's theory and liberalism, the broader capability approach that extends beyond Sen is compatible with a range of political traditions. Robeyns (2016) states that liberalism is not a part of the core of the capability approach, and suggests that a different ethical idea of normative individualism is instead part of this core. This refers to the idea that the individual should be at the centre of any moral theory. Different ethical ideas are compatible with the commitment to normative individualism. These theories can range from libertarian to egalitarian ideas. She writes that it is 'logically possible to develop a right–libertarian capability theory that understands fairness and justice very differently from the egalitarian and strongly redistributive account of social justice that is favoured in the existing capability literature' (Robeyns, 2016: 402). Robeyn's (2016) claim means that the capability approach does not necessarily support social citizenship. For example, public policy might only use a capability theory to support civil or political rights. Much depends on how capability theory is developed. Sen's capability theory does support a redistributive agenda and so offers a possible basis for social citizenship.

The capability approach and poverty

Supporters of Sen's capability theory make a direct link between this and anti-poverty policy (Johnson and Sherraden, 2007; McQuaid and Edgell, 2010; Balakrishnan et al, 2011; Storchi and Johnson, 2016). McQuaid and Edgell (2010: 19) comment that the 'wider capability approach (developed by Amartya Sen ...), within which financial capability can be seen to fit ... is becoming more commonly used in anti-poverty strategies'. This quotation makes two claims: first, that the capability approach is important for anti-poverty policy; and, second, that financial capability is part of the capability approach. This chapter now considers each of these claims.

There are two main traditions for analysing poverty within social policy. These are the 'direct' and 'indirect' traditions of anti-poverty analysis. A direct tradition focuses on the standard of living experienced by people (Hick, 2012; Deeming, 2017; Davis et al, 2018). Indirect theories of poverty concentrate instead on the resources possessed by individuals, particularly on levels of income. If people fall below a poverty income level, then they are viewed as being in poverty. Hick (2012) argues that the capability approach contributes to a direct tradition of poverty analysis. He highlights that the 'capability approach offers a framework for poverty analysis which prioritises capabilities (ends) over resources (means), adopts a multidimensional perspective and takes a broad focus on the constraints that may restrict human lives' (Hick, 2012: 301). Hick (2012) suggests that the capability approach makes several contributions to the analysis of poverty. First, it makes a distinction between means and ends. In particular, what matters are the ends of anti-poverty policy rather than the means needed to achieve those ends. Supporters of the capability approach claim that the stress should be on capabilities and functionings rather than the contingent means that are used to achieve these ends. For example, money is likely to be important for supporting both capabilities and functionings. However, money is just a means and what demands attention are the actual capabilities or functionings. Second, the capability approach recognises that there are a range of worthwhile ends rather than a single valuable end. A variety of capabilities are important and so there are different facets to poverty. Third, the role of capabilities and functionings recognises that people face wider constraints.

Sen (1985, 1998, 2009) does not prescribe a fixed set of capabilities. Rather, he suggests that they may vary over time and be shaped by democratic debate. Financial capability and the capability approach share a label. However, a common label does not necessarily mean that the former is necessarily part of the latter. The most promising overlaps between financial capability and the capability approach appear to occur for those models that emphasise financial knowledge.

The capacity to make financial decisions might be deemed a worthwhile part of citizenship. Arguably, any satisfactory notion of social citizenship has to refer to resources as well as the capacity to make financial choices. The capability approach highlights that people need resources to be able to develop capabilities or functionings. Money is likely to be important for any meaningful sense of financial capability. Making financial decisions is likely to be fairly meaningless if people have the capacity and motivation to make choices, have access to the financial system, but do not have any money to make these choices. Any opportunities that people experience will then be formal rather than real. Thus, three things seem to be important, namely, money, financial capability and financial inclusion. Some commentators might prefer to stress the provision of money over the other items. For example, governments might concentrate on ensuring that people and households have enough money rather than taking steps to boost financial capability. However, these different aspects are not mutually exclusive and governments might seek to boost income and wealth as well as to enhance financial capability and inclusion.

Building financial capability

One debate concerns the best way to build financial capability. Much of this discussion centres on the contribution that financial education or behavioural nudges may play in boosting financial capability. Financial education appears to be an obvious way of trying to build financial capability. Lusardi (2019: 6) argues that 'Financial education is a crucial foundation for raising financial literacy and informing the next generation of consumers, workers and citizens.'

This view is not accepted by all scholars. Willis (2008, 2011) argues that there is an important 'financial education fallacy', which is made up of two parts. First, she questions whether financial education improves financial knowledge. Willis (2008, 2011) argues that most empirical studies into financial education are poorly designed, for example, there are studies that rely on the self-reported perceptions of people who have attended financial education courses. She argues that there is a bias in these studies because those people who undertook the course have an incentive to report that it improved their financial knowledge regardless of whether or not this was actually the case. Willis (2008, 2011) says that there is a lack of properly designed randomised control trials in this empirical literature that compares a 'treatment' group that received financial education with a 'control' group that did not receive the education.

Second, Willis (2008, 2011) claims that even if financial education can be shown to improve financial knowledge, there is little evidence to suggest that increased knowledge prompts a change in behaviour. She suggests that it would be better to explore alternatives to financial education as a way of changing behaviour. Willis (2011) proposes two alternatives to financial education to help consumers within financial markets. First, governments may pay for independent financial advisers for consumers. Second, governments might implement behavioural nudges to change behaviour: 'Another possibility is to abandon trying to change people and instead harness their biases to work in favor of welfare-enhancing financial "decisions". Retirement savings defaults have been more effective than retirement savings education, and they cost little to put in place' (Willis, 2011: 432).

Willis (2008, 2011) is probably the most trenchant critic of financial education. One might contest her claims over financial education. Research exists which suggests that there are properly designed empirical studies which highlight that financial education improves financial knowledge (Heinberg et al, 2014; Lusardi et al, 2017, 2019). Heinberg et al (2014: 698) contend that 'A key next step is therefore to move beyond a potentially misleading discussion of *whether* "generic" financial education works, towards an understanding of how to make financial education work through better design and appropriate delivery methods.' Research from the US has suggested that video stories and financial technology delivered through the web can improve financial literacy and self-efficacy, thereby potentially leading to improved decisions (Lusardi et al, 2017). Heinberg et al (2014) report results on the impact of YouTube videos and written narratives on a five-step plan for boosting financial planning. These five steps focus on knowledge of five key concepts for retirement planning, namely, compound interest, inflation, risk diversification, tax treatment of retirement savings and employer matches of defined contribution schemes. In the five-step experiment, financial literacy is measured before and after the video and narrative treatments, and is compared with a control group. Financial literacy is measured through a survey used in international assessments of financial literacy (Lusardi and Mitchell, 2011; Heinberg et al, 2014). Lusardi et al (2017) extend the work of Heinberg et al (2014) by considering the impact of an expanded set of online tools (for example, an interactive visual tool) alongside a video, information brochure and written narrative. Lusardi et al (2017) state that the video had most impact but call for more research into the impact of more interactive visual tools that are easy to access. Such tools might be delivered through smartphones.

Behavioural nudges

Willis (2011) proposes behavioural nudges as an alternative to financial education. This reflects a growing interest in behavioural economics and public policy. Thaler and Sunstein's (2008) book *Nudge* kick-started much of the recent interest in behavioural economics (Camerer and Loewenstein, 2004; Thaler and Sunstein, 2008; House of Lords Science and Technology Select Committee, 2011; John et al, 2011; Oliver, 2013, 2015; Jones et al, 2014).

Altman (2012) distinguishes between two main strands of behavioural economics. The first is an 'error and biases' approach that is rooted in the work of scholars such as Kahneman and Tversky (1979). This strand highlights the common psychological biases exhibited by individuals. There is a range of biases that are cited in this literature, such as loss aversion (where people prefer to avoid losses than make gains), overconfidence and herding (where people tend to follow the crowd). Kahneman (2011: 300) writes that the 'concept of loss aversion is certainly the most significant contribution of psychology to behavioral economics'. The 'errors and biases' approach highlights a distinction between automatic or 'type 1' thinking and controlled or 'type 2' thinking (Schneider and Shiffrin, 1977; Camerer et al, 2004, 2005; Camerer, 2007; Kahneman, 2011). Automatic processes are those brain activities that occur quickly without much deliberation. Controlled processes are those things that require logic and computation. Many of the biases have their roots in automatic rather than controlled thinking.

The second strand of behavioural economics is a 'fast and frugal' approach based on work in bounded rationality. Herbert Simon (1955) is one of the pioneers of this approach. Simon (1955) claims that the standard economic model of decision-making is flawed because it rests on unrealistic assumptions about the capacity or people to absorb and compute the information needed to make decisions that maximise individual welfare. He argues that there are limits on calculation. His aim is to 'replace the global rationality or economic man with a kind of rational behaviour that is compatible with the access to information and the computational capacities that are actually possessed by organisms, including man, in the kinds of environments in which organisms exist' (Simon, 1955: 99). Altman (2012) argues that this branch of behavioural economics highlights the significance of people applying shortcuts or 'heuristics' to make decisions. People might exhibit status quo bias as a useful shortcut to processing a lot of information. People may find that it takes too much time and effort to compute this information and that it is easier and simpler to stick to the status quo.

Altman (2012) argues that these different parts of behavioural economics have different implications for financial education. He argues that the 'errors and biases' strand suggests that financial education is likely to have little effect on behaviour as these biases are 'hard-wired' into people. He argues that it is better for policymakers to try and use these biases to promote certain types of behaviour. Altman (2012) says that financial education may be more useful in the 'fast and frugal' approach. He says that the latter implies that the design of institutions is important for shaping people to make particular choices. However, he claims that financial education can improve the information that people have when making choices within a particular institutional context, for example:

> Financial education can play a role in changing savings behaviour from the perspective of bounded rationality, but not by changing the behavioural traits of decision makers. Rather, by providing employees with improved information, it is possible that some employees will choose to invest more towards their retirement. Also, providing information on pension plan options can allow employees to better understand the risks involved in particular pension plans. (Altman, 2012: 683)

An example: Save More Tomorrow

Altman (2012) suggests that financial education and behavioural economics might be usefully combined in steps to boost retirement saving. This is one of the most important applications of behavioural economics ideas. This section looks more closely at this example, looking particularly at the Save More Tomorrow (SMarT) scheme. Designing the default is arguably the main proposal to emerge from behavioural economics (Willis, 2013). Willis (2013: 1157) says that '"Nudging" – framing people's choices so as to channel them to better outcomes without substantively limiting choice – is all the rage, and perhaps the most popular framing tool is the use of policy defaults.' A tendency of people to stick to the status quo is a core reason for the weight placed on setting the default. As Thaler and Sunstein (2008: 8–9) note: 'consider what is called the "status quo bias", a fancy name for inertia. For a host of reasons, which we shall explore, people have a strong tendency to go along with the status quo or default option.'

One area where status quo bias is applied is on plans to boost private saving for retirement. Thaler and Sunstein (2008) question the main life-cycle approach used within standard economic theory. According to life-cycle theory, people save money when they are working in order to pay for consumption once they are retired. People design a savings plan to smooth consumption over their lifetime (Attansio et al, 2005; Crawford et al, 2012).

Thaler and Sunstein (2008) argue that there are two key problems with such life-cycle models. First, people find it almost impossible to design an optimal lifetime savings plan. Ring (2012) claims that the complexity of making pension choices creates difficulties for people to make any sort of rational decision at all. Ring (2012) argues that uncertainty over pension outcomes and the risks of pension investment mean that trust is important in pension decisions. He adds that AE may make trust more important as more people will be switched into defined contribution schemes and so people will have to trust that employers and financial institutions will provide suitable schemes.

Second, Thaler and Sunstein (2008) argue that even if people can design an optimal savings plan, people find it difficult to stick to such a plan. People have a range of competing demands at different points of their life, such as student debt or housing costs, and this may mean that retirement savings are not always a priority (Creedy et al, 2015; Foster, 2017). Existing work also suggests that planning for a pension is related to age, with people not thinking much about pension provision until their 30s or 40s, and women thinking about this later than men (MacLeod et al, 2012; Scottish Widows, 2020).

Thaler and colleagues propose that governments ought to shape the architecture of choice to encourage more saving for retirement (Thaler and Benartzi, 2004, 2007; Thaler and Sunstein, 2008). They highlight four key biases when thinking about pension saving:

> bounded rationality, self-control, procrastination (which produces inertia), and nominal loss aversion. These households are not sure how much they should be saving, though they realize that it is probably more than they are

doing now; but they procrastinate about saving more now, thinking that they will get to it later. (Thaler and Benartzi, 2004: 170)

Thaler and Benartzi (2004, 2007) designed the SMarT programme based on these behavioural biases. SMarT has two main parts: first, people are automatically enrolled into a pension; and, second, members then save at a default rate. Status quo bias means that people will tend to remain enrolled in the pension and save at the default rate (Thaler and Benartzi, 2004, 2007; Thaler and Sunstein, 2008). Rising contributions into a pension should be tied to wage rises to mitigate the effect of loss aversion. Employees are free to opt out at any time.

Do behavioural nudges undermine freedom?

The preceding discussion suggests that financial capability might be used to support a capability approach. Furthermore, Sen's capability theory could be used to enhance social citizenship. The preceding discussion has also considered debates about whether financial education or behavioural nudges are better placed to build financial capability. Education is usually an important part of a capability approach. However, behavioural nudges create a potential issue as there are debates about the ethics of behavioural nudges.

Supporters of behavioural economics argue that it respects liberal principles. Thaler and Sunstein (2008) claim that their nudge theory is a type of 'libertarian paternalism'. They state that:

> We strive to design policies that maintain or increase freedom of choice. When we use the term *libertarian* to modify the word *paternalism*, we simply mean liberty-preserving. And when we say liberty-preserving, we really mean it. Libertarian paternalists want to make it easy for people to go their own way; they do not want to burden those who want to exercise their freedom. (Thaler and Sunstein, 2008: 5, emphasis in original)

Thaler and Sunstein (2008) say that their theory is paternalist as it involves the government setting the context for individual choices. The government sets the choice architecture that tries to nudge people to make particular choices. Thaler and Sunstein (2008) state that the final decision rests with the individual. This means that nudge theory preserves freedom of choice and so can be dubbed libertarian.

Hausman and Welch (2010) question whether nudge theory is genuinely libertarian. They argue that paternalism usually involves governments limiting the choices available to individuals. Hausman and Welch (2010) continue that nudge theory does not try to limit the set of choices available to individuals and so is not a usual type of paternalism. They say that nudge theory can be seen as paternalist insofar as the government shapes individual choices. They write that:

> We shall call the use of flaws in human decision-making to get individuals to choose one alternative rather than another 'shaping' their choices. We intend 'shaping' to exclude rational persuasion. 'Manipulation' would be a more natural label, but since we are concerned with whether shaping people's choices is justified, we have avoided using a word with such pejorative connotations. (Hausman and Welch, 2010: 128–9)

Although Hausman and Welch (2010) avoid the term 'manipulation', it has nevertheless been used in ethical debates about nudge theory (Thaler and Sunstein, 2008; Bovens, 2009; Wilkinson, 2013). Manipulation raises ethical issues as it may undermine individual autonomy, that is, the control that people have over their own choices. For this reason, Hausman and Welch (2010) question whether nudge theory is really libertarian. Other commentators suggest that transparency over the presence of a nudge, as well as easy and fairly costless opportunities to opt out from the nudge, may be enough to protect people from manipulation (Bovens, 2009; Wilkinson, 2013).

Thaler and Sunstein (2008) support a publicity principle that would make people aware of the presence of a nudge. As they say:

> Consider Save More Tomorrow; here people are explicitly informed of the nature of the proposal, and specifically asked whether they would like to accept it. Similarly, when firms adopt automatic enrolment, they do not make a secret of it, and can say honestly that they do so because they think that most workers will be better off joining the plan. (Thaler and Sunstein, 2008: 245)

Thaler and Sunstein (2008) suggest that making workers aware of SMarT nudges, as well as giving opportunities for them to opt out from its provisions, is enough to protect employees from the possibility of manipulation.

Tensions between behavioural economics and activity

Early examples of AE occurred within particular companies in the US. Studies into these schemes suggest that AE can boost the membership of a workplace pension (Madrian and Shea, 2001; Choi et al, 2002, 2004). In one of the most cited studies into this policy, Madrian and Shea (2001) report evidence from a US health employer that changed its pension scheme from a voluntary opt-in scheme to AE. They note that when the scheme required people to opt out, those participating in the scheme went from 48.7 per cent of old members to 85.9 per cent of the new cohort. Madrian and Shea (2001) argue that their results show the 'power of suggestion', that is, participation in a workplace pension scheme is suggested by AE. They say that procrastination is an important factor behind the power of suggestion. They call for more research into the factors behind the power of suggestion, and comment that if procrastination emerges because of complexity in making savings decisions, then policymakers should explore how to make such decisions simpler. They contend that if procrastination occurs because people lack proper information or advice about AE, then education may be a better response.

Madrian and Shea (2001) raise a general point about the best way to change behaviour. Behavioural nudges focus on attitudes or motivations rather than financial knowledge. Although doubts have been cast over the impact of financial education on changing behaviour, behavioural nudges raise their own issues. The assumptions that are used to justify behavioural nudges might also lead to limitations. This can be seen in the use of SMarT techniques to boost saving. Thaler and Benartzi (2004: 169) acknowledge that there is a 'downside to automatic enrollment. The very inertia that explains why automatic enrollment increases participation rates can also lower the savings rates of those who do participate.' Lack of activity may be a problem because the default savings rate may not guarantee an adequate income in retirement for all of the population. People might be expected to save beyond the default savings rate, which means the need for activity.

This tension between activity and passivity is also noted in a UK government review of AE. AE will be examined further in Chapter 3. However, in 2016, the UK government convened a review of AE to consider the next steps for this policy. The final report of this review was published on 17 December 2017 (Department for Work and Pensions, 2017). Boosting individual engagement with workplace pensions is one of the three key strategic challenges discussed by this review: 'By defaulting individuals into saving and harnessing their natural inertia, automatic enrolment is changing the behaviour of millions of people and is turning them into savers. However, many individuals are not yet engaged with their pension saving' (Department for Work and Pensions, 2017: 73).

The review states that there was often little engagement with private pension saving prior to AE. It says that many of the barriers to pension saving that existed before are still in place and this is why AE is still needed, highlighting a number of issues that need to be addressed:

> Behavioural analysis tells us that when faced with decisions around pensions, individual procrastinate. ... The real or perceived complexity of pensions, including choice overload, can deter individuals from making decisions. This challenge of complexity may be further exacerbated by low levels of literacy and numeracy and by the fragmentation of individual's savings into more than one pension pot. (Department for Work and Pensions, 2017: 75)

The previous quotation notes that people procrastinate. However, this procrastination is linked to the difficulty in making pension decisions. An obvious response to this is to try and help people cope with this complexity. The quotation mentions low literacy and numeracy, and so one response is for government to try and boost financial education. This may be a more direct answer to procrastination than trying to design further behavioural nudges.

The review also cites other factors: 'some responses to the Review have suggested that individuals may be distrustful of pensions and financial services. Mistrust may combine with misconceptions that discourage saving' (Department for Work and Pensions, 2017: 75). Again, these factors are arguably less about innate cognitive limits than rational responses to problems within financial services. Governments might be better off concentrating on the greater regulation of financial services rather than looking for more nudges.

Conclusion

This chapter has examined financial capability. This topic is important because if people are to make financial decisions, then they need the capacity and motivation to make financial choices, as well as access to the financial system. This area is also relevant for financialisation as critics present financial capability as part of the effort to create investor-subjects. This chapter claimed that financial capability can be used to create investor-subjects. The chapter also suggested that financial capability might be used to support citizenship. It argued that the most promising route for the latter is by seeing financial capability as part of a capability approach. Such a stance ought to acknowledge that people and households need money as well as financial capability and financial inclusion. Governments should therefore ensure that people and households have money alongside any steps to bolster financial capability. This book will return to this point in Chapter 5 when it looks at ideas such as basic income as a way of providing people with regular income payments.

The chapter also considered different ways of building financial capability and reflected on the role played by financial education and behavioural nudges. Although these different approaches are sometimes presented as being opposites, there are reasons to try and combine these approaches. This chapter considered this with the example of the SMarT saving scheme. The next chapter picks up some of these themes when it examines financial inclusion and saving. One of the areas to be explored is the automatic enrolment into a workplace pension in the UK, which was influenced by SMarT ideas.

3

Financial inclusion and saving

Introduction

The opening chapters have introduced the concepts of financial inclusion and financial capability. These chapters have presented financial inclusion and financial capability as complementary. If people are to make financial decisions, then they need access to the financial system. This points to the significance of financial inclusion. However, people also need to be able to make financial decisions once they are connected to the 'financial mains' but may lack the knowledge, skills or confidence to do so. Furthermore, the capacity to make financial decisions might be deemed an important part of individual freedom. This highlights the significance of financial capability.

This chapter turns from the general discussions in earlier chapters to a study of what financial inclusion might mean in practice. Studying concrete examples of financial inclusion can add flesh to the general discussion of financial inclusion, as well as highlight some of the dilemmas and challenges faced by financial inclusion. There are a wide range of areas that it is possible to study. Chapter 1 mentioned that financial inclusion covers areas such as banking, insurance, credit and savings. There is also a varied range of policies within each of these different sectors. It is not possible to survey all the possible areas of interest. Rather, this chapter concentrates on financial inclusion savings policies as it is a particular area of policy concern in the UK. Data exist which suggest that important parts of the population have little or no savings. For example, around 53 per cent of 22 to 29 year olds in the UK had no savings at all in a savings account between 2014 and 2016. The UK's housing saving ratio – that is, savings as a proportion of household income – halved between 2015 and 2018. The UK's household savings ratio is also lower than the average across the European Union (McKay et al, 2019).

The UK government has sought to address this lack of saving. For example, former Labour Chancellor Alistair Darling promised a Saving Gateway policy would be introduced from 2010 to boost saving. These would be special two-year savings accounts aimed at those on low incomes in which the government would match 50p for every £1 saved by a Saving Gateway account holder (with a maximum of £25 of government contributions each month) (House of Commons Library, 2009; HM Treasury, 2010a). The Saving Gateway, as well as the CTF (considered later), were casualties of the first wave of spending cuts announced by the incoming Conservative–Liberal Democrat Coalition government after the 2010 general election. These were part of the austerity cuts to public spending. The planned national roll-out of the Saving Gateway was cancelled and the government stopped making payments into the CTF in 2011.

Despite this, these initiatives have not disappeared. The Saving Gateway still attracts support among the policy community in the UK (Financial Inclusion Commission, 2015). After the 2015 general election, Conservative Chancellor George Osborne revived the Saving Gateway with the introduction of his 'Help to Save' scheme announced in his 2016 Budget. The Help to Save scheme is available to those 3.5 million adults in receipt of Working Tax Credit or Universal Credit with minimum weekly household earnings equivalent to 16 hours at the National Living Wage. There is a 50 per cent government bonus paid after two years on savings of up to £50 a month in the Help to Save account. Therefore, personal savings of £2,400 would attract a £1,200 government bonus (HM Treasury, 2016). There are also calls for the CTF to be revived (Atkinson, 2015).

This chapter looks more closely at two policies aimed at encouraging people to build long-term saving, namely, the CTF and automatic enrolment into a workplace pension. Both are pioneering examples of savings policies. The CTF was aimed at ensuring that all young people had access to savings when they turned 18 years old. Automatic enrolment into a workplace pension is intended to support private savings for retirement.

The lifespan of the CTF was fairly short. Nevertheless, the CTF offers useful insights for the design of financial inclusion. The CTF has been cited as an exemplar of asset-based welfare. One of the criticisms of the CTF was that it was ultimately aimed at creating investor-subjects (Watson, 2008; Finlayson, 2009). As Finlayson (2009: 409) argues: 'Asset-based welfare policies, as implemented by New Labour, do not have as their primary goal the redistribution of wealth but rather the incorporation of individuals within the mainstream financial system ... and the opening up of opportunities to enhance financial literacy.' This chapter argues that although this criticism of the Labour government's CTF has some force, it nonetheless overlooks different ways that the policy was developing in different parts of the UK. In particular, the devolved Welsh government shaped the CTF in ways that supported an alternative and more egalitarian agenda.

The future for the automatic enrolment into a workplace pension is more promising. As the Financial Inclusion Commission (2015: 17) says:

> Auto-enrolment workplace pension schemes are being set up across the country and will have to be offered by all employers by 2018. Because workers are automatically enrolled onto a scheme and will have to opt out, this change should greatly increase the take up of pension savings. It will mean that millions of people who have never before saved for their retirement start to do so. This is a positive step in helping people to build financial resilience.

The Financial Inclusion Commission (2015) recommends that AE be implemented for other workplace savings products. This chapter discusses original qualitative research into the workings of this policy. The findings highlight the challenges that should be faced if financial inclusion is to be shaped in a more egalitarian direction.

The chapter is organised as follows. The first section sketches out asset-based welfare as this provides much of the rationale for the CTF. The second part outlines a criticism that the CTF was aimed at creating investor-subjects in financial markets. The third segment points to the different ways that the CTF was developing in the UK. This looks specifically at the Welsh government's reforms of the CTF. This discussion is important as it highlights the different ways that it is possible to design financial inclusion policies. The chapter then moves on to consider the automatic enrolment into a workplace pension. The chapter then discusses the limitations of AE and suggests issues that ought to be addressed with the policy.

Asset-based welfare

Asset-based welfare provided much of the rationale for the CTF and the Saving Gateway. The US academic Michael Sherraden coined the term 'asset-based welfare' during the 1990s to refer to a new approach to social policy that stresses the importance of the individual ownership of assets such as pensions or savings (Sherraden, 1990, 1991, 2003; Schreiner et al, 2002; McKernan and Sherraden, 2008). His ideas were set out most fully in his 1991 book *Assets and the Poor. A New American Welfare Policy* (Sherraden, 1991), with the title of his book making a direct link between assets and the poor and, by so doing, highlighting that his theory is part of a social policy tradition that focuses on tackling poverty.

The 'asset effect' is central to asset-based welfare. Sherraden (1991) argues that transfers of income through the tax and benefit system are the main way that social policy addresses poverty. He states that income transfers relieve the symptoms but do not address the underlying causes of poverty. Sherraden (1991) argues that assets are fundamentally different from income as they are a stock variable, whereas income is a flow variable. Nam, Huang and Sherraden (2008: 2) state that 'Stocks of assets in the context of social policy are usually in the form of financial wealth (e.g. subsidies for retirement accounts or educational savings accounts) or tangible wealth (e.g. subsidies for homeownership)'. Sherraden (1991) claims that providing people with a stock of assets creates an 'asset effect' over and above the provision of income that causes people to think and behave differently in the world. People then take the steps to avoid problems from occurring. For example, people may invest in training to avoid possible redundancy.

Sherraden (2003) makes a link between asset-based welfare and Sen's capability approach (discussed in Chapter 2). He says that the 'best social policy alternatives will move beyond the idea of consumption-as-well-being, toward what Sen ... identifies as functionings or capabilities. Building people's assets is one policy pathway to both increase capabilities and improve the trade-off between economic growth and social development' (Sherraden 2003). Nam, Huang and Sherraden (2008) argue that Sen does not specify the capacities that need to be developed. These researchers argue that it is important to specify and test different capacities. They say that asset-based welfare offers an opportunity to add more detail to the capability approach.

Three factors might contribute to an asset effect: first, this effect might emerge from holding the asset; second, the process of acquiring or building the asset might prompt a change in the way that people think or behave; and, third, an asset effect might emerge from the way that an asset is used (Bynner and Paxton, 2001; McKernan and Sherraden, 2008). The relative contribution of the different factors may vary for different assets. The mix of these different causes is important for designing asset policies. For example, if acquiring assets is the main cause of the asset effect, then policies should support the acquisition rather than the holding or use of assets.

The asset effect hypothesis is controversial. Although there is a growing empirical literature that confirms the presence of such an effect, this is not accepted by all commentators. Furthermore, there is a critique that casts doubt on whether assets are the best means of achieving the desired policy outcomes. For example, improving individual skills might be better achieved through more public spending on schools or colleges rather than encouraging individual investments into IDAs (see Bynner and Despotidou, 2000; Bynner and Paxton, 2001; Emmerson and Wakefield, 2001; Loke and Sacco, 2011; Gregory, 2014).

IDAs

Sherraden (1991) pioneered IDAs to embody asset-based welfare. These are special savings accounts that are targeted at those on low incomes. Personal savings into these accounts attract matching contributions from private agencies (such as corporations) or public bodies (such as the central government or local authorities). A cap is usually placed on the matched contributions. The lifespan for IDAs can vary but they may last for several years. Sherraden (1991) proposed that savings into these accounts should be used for individual development, in particular, to start a business, pay for training or put down a deposit on a home (Sherraden, 1990, 1991, 2003; Schreiner et al, 2002; McKernan and Sherraden, 2008).

IDAs have prompted much interest. Sherraden helped to found the Center for Social Development at the University of Washington at St Louis, which coordinates and shares research into IDAs across the world. There have been trials or pilots of IDAs in countries such as the US and Uganda. In the US, there is an empirical literature studying the impact of IDAs on the savings of those on low incomes. An early study was an American Dream Demonstration programme than ran from 1997 to 2001. A final report into this programme found that poorer people were able to save into IDAs. The average participant saved around US$1 for every US$2 that could be matched and they made a deposit in about six of every 12 months (Schreiner et al, 2002). There have since been a range of studies carried out on related initiatives, such as child development accounts or college savings funds, and so there is a US literature on financial inclusion and savings policies (McKernan and Sherraden, 2008).

Feldman (2018) provides a critical review of the empirical literature on IDAs. He examines what existing research reveals as regards three questions, namely: whether IDAs boost savings; whether they change their clients' outlooks on life; and what the general impact of IDAs is on the accumulation of assets. He says that a common feature of these studies is a lack of properly designed randomised control trials that compare a control group with a group that has an IDA treatment. He argues that a critical review of this literature suggests only weak empirical support for the impacts of IDAs.

Feldman (2018) continues that asset-based welfare has important shortcomings for the study of poverty. First, asset-based welfare and IDAs prioritise individual agency rather than structure as a cause of poverty. Poverty is seen as emerging from individual failings rather than wider inequalities. Second, he casts doubt on the emphasis on home-ownership in IDAs. He argues that the experience of the global financial crisis suggests that the drive to home-ownership might worsen rather than resolve problems. Third, Feldman (2018) questions whether higher education is a path to higher wages. He says that this ignores the extent to which there is a lack of jobs that pay decent wages. He claims that these are different facets of a neoliberal approach to welfare: 'Asset-building initiatives articulate a neoliberal logic since their role is to re-fashion people into disciplined market actors who save and accumulate capital so as to enhance their own capacities and better compete in a market-centred society' (Feldman, 2018: 187).

Feldman (2018) does not reject asset-based welfare in its entirety. Rather, he points to ways in which this agenda might be recast. For example, he proposes that asset-based welfare might be used to open up new debates about home-ownership that point to more collectively owned assets. This book will examine the issue of housing further in Chapter 4. Feldman (2018: 195) states that rather than teaching people how to be:

> good solo participants in the prevailing mainstream capitalist economy, asset-building can help clients act collectively via alternative forms of banking such as credit unions and cooperatives, which do not engage in predatory practices that sometimes turn people's dreams of upward mobility into a nightmare. It can also counter the capriciousness of the private housing market by promoting affordable housing that is funded and regulated by the government.

He also calls for more qualitative research into how people engage with asset-based policies and poverty policies more generally. He suggests that this can gain a deeper insight into the structural constraints that shape the lives of those living in poverty. This chapter addresses this point later when it reports original qualitative research into the automatic enrolment into a workplace pension.

Long-term saving: the CTF

In 2005, the Labour government introduced the CTF. This provided all babies born in the UK from September 2002 with £250, with an extra £250 going to children from low-income backgrounds. The extra top-ups for children from low-income families were part of 'progressive universalism', that is, grants for all with extra endowments for those most in need. These endowments were paid into 18-year accounts and up to £1,200 could be saved into these accounts each year (HM Treasury, 2003).

Sherraden was specifically invited by the Labour government to contribute to the development of the CTF in the run-up to this policy announcement. A prototype of the CTF was modelled on Sherraden's IDAs (Kelly and Lissauer, 2000). Research by Bynner and Despotidou (2000) on the asset effect was influential for calculating the size of the initial endowment into the CTF. Their research used the UK National Child Development Survey to show that modest amounts of financial wealth (of around several hundred pounds) was enough to create an asset effect that would lead to improvements in personal outcomes (such as better health).

The CTF involved paying a capital grant to all babies. This attracted the support of reformists, who saw this as an opportunity to implement a redistributive agenda. This overlaps with the 'basic capital' agenda that will be examined in Chapter 5. However, supporters of a basic capital agenda usually called for a much larger endowment for all young people. For example, Le Grand and Nissan (2000) call for a £10,000 grant to be paid to all young people at age 18. The small endowment in the CTF disappointed reformists. They saw the radical potential of this policy being overwhelmed by Labour's emphasis on using the CTF to support a savings culture. The importance of the savings culture for the policy can be seen by the fact that Labour embedded the CTF in its strategy on saving, as outlined in 'Saving and assets for all' and 'Delivering saving and assets' (HM Treasury, 2001a, 2001b). These consultation documents argue that Labour saw plans for asset-based welfare as a new leg of the welfare state, alongside work and skills, income benefits, and public services (HM Treasury, 2001a). Labour also wanted to combine the CTF with financial education in schools. Critics argued that the CTF was ultimately used to support an investor-subject approach rather than offer a more radical attack on wealth inequality (Watson, 2008; Finlayson, 2008, 2009).

Discussion

Although Labour's approach to the CTF stressed the importance of personal responsibility and saving, there were also parts of the policy that drew on egalitarian arguments. The extra £250 to children from lower-income families introduced the notion of 'progressive universalism'. Gordon Brown introduced this term when he was Chancellor of the Exchequer in 2002 (Gregory and Drakeford, 2011). Progressive universalism means a commitment to universal services with extra progressive help for those most in need. In the *Pre Budget Report 2002*, progressive universalism was applied mainly to the CTF:

> The CTF would be a universal account, opened for all children at birth, with an endowment paid by the Government. Founded on the principle of progressive universalism, every child would receive an endowment, with those from the poorest families receiving the largest lump sums. The CTF would advance the Government's goal to promote saving opportunity by ensuring that all young adults, regardless of their families' circumstances, start their adult lives with immediate access to a stock of assets. (HM Treasury, 2002: 98)

Labour's steps on progressive universalism were outweighed by its emphasis on saving. The dominant approach Labour took to the CTF meant that, in practice, the overall effect of the policy as it stood might increase inequality. First, higher-income families are better placed to save into the CTF than lower-income families. The CTF allowed family and friends to save up to £1,200 a year into these accounts. Official statistics show that for children born between 1 September 2002 and 5 April 2010, 13 per cent of the CTFs of those from lower-income families had further savings compared to 28 per cent of the CTFs of children from better-off backgrounds. The average saving in the CTFs of better-off children was also higher, with an average of £321 being saved a year compared to £181 into the accounts of children from lower-income backgrounds (HM Revenue and Customs, 2011). This means that the overall effect of the CTF could increase inequality without some special measures targeted at those on low incomes.

Second, since the financial crisis of the late 2000s, real interest rates on savings have often been minimal or negative. This raises the question of whether people should be encouraged into making long-term savings in a policy such as the CTF. A counter to this highlights the risk of having no savings at all.

However, upon maturity, the CTF provides all 18 year olds with a modest cushion that they can access instantly. Those who get the top-up have £500 in their CTF. If no further savings are made into the CTF, then the real value of this endowment will fall over 18 years. If annual inflation is 2 per cent (the government's inflation target) and no interest is paid on the £500, then the real value of the endowment upon maturity falls to £350. This could still provide a modest financial cushion, though it then raises the question of whether the endowment might be better provided directly when the person is 18 rather than giving this at birth.

Third, there is debate as to whether policy should concentrate on boosting incomes rather than assets during the early years of a child's life. Research suggests that the financial constraints facing families, particularly women, tend to be greatest when children are very young (Ginn and Arber, 2002; Women's Budget Group, 2010). This raises a question of whether a better policy for reducing poverty would be boosting income by increasing Child Benefit rather than the CTF. The Child Poverty Action Group (2005) argues that while it supported the idea embodied in the CTF of giving help to families with young children, it would have preferred to see an increase in Child Benefit. One response from supporters of the CTF is that there is no necessary trade-off between the CTF and Child Benefit. Sherraden (1991) argues that policy should embrace income replacement and assets. He argues that asset ownership is aimed at stopping poverty being reproduced across the generations and so has a role alongside income replacement. One response to this is that although there is no necessary trade-off, policy nevertheless has to maximise impact with limited resources. A choice therefore exists between Child Benefit and the CTF. One might question how policy choices are framed though. White (2010) suggests that a capital endowment might fare better if compared to a different choice, say against subsidies for higher education. Nonetheless, questions can be asked about whether the CTF is the best way of securing progressive ends.

Fourth, the CTF could have added to weaknesses in financial services under Labour. Labour presented the CTF as a 'stakeholder' saving product aimed at those on low and middle incomes. A 1 per cent cap was usually applied to the fees that could be charged on stakeholder products. Financial service providers argued that a 1 per cent cap would be too low to offer them an incentive to provide CTFs (Select Committee on Treasury, 2003). A 1.5 per cent management fee cap was eventually agreed. Although the 1.5 per cent cap might reflect successful rent-seeking by financial services, the CTF was nevertheless not seen by financial services as a premium product. Financial institutions were generally able to use pooled CTF funds as part of their wider activities. Although it is possible to have a system that separates the retail and investment functions of banks (Independent Commission on Banking, 2011), no firewall existed under Labour. The CTF allowed access to funds that could be used for financial speculation. However, certain institutions were more responsible for the crisis than others. For example, the Royal Bank of Scotland and Northern Rock played a bigger role than many other institutions (see the discussion of credit unions later) (Independent Commission on Banking, 2011).

The Welsh government reforms

The preceding discussion suggests that there are valid concerns about the CTF. Arguably, Labour used the policy to stress personal responsibility rather than equality. Indeed, it is likely that the policy would worsen rather than reduce inequality. Therefore, there is substance in the charge that Labour's CTF was largely embedded in an investor-subject approach. Although this criticism of Labour has force, this is not the complete story. There were countervailing parts of the CTF that pointed this policy in other directions. This section now suggests that policy elsewhere in the UK pushed the CTF further in these other directions. In particular, the Welsh government adapted the CTF and, in doing so, highlighted that it is possible to design policies in different ways.

Devolved government in the UK provides the context which ensured that differences in the CTF policy could emerge. In the late 1990s, the UK government at Westminster created devolved administrations in Scotland, Wales and Northern Ireland. The Westminster government dominates the devolved state in the UK, for example, with the control it has in setting national budget settlements. Nevertheless, the different devolved governments have flexibility in implementing and shaping policy.

Williams and Mooney (2008) argue that devolution creates space for different social policy agendas to emerge in the UK. This section argues that the Welsh government took a policy that applied across the UK – the CTF – and made changes that pushed it in a direction different from that adopted by New Labour in Westminster. Part of this involved extending certain parts of the policy further than in the rest of the UK, that is, its commitment to progressive universalism.

Part of this introduced novel twists, specifically using the government to support the delivery of the CTF through credit unions.

Progressive universalism

Progressive universalism was one of the features of the UK-wide CTF. One distinct feature of the Welsh government's approach was the priority it placed on this part of the CTF over that of the rest of the UK. The main way that this occurred was through the Welsh government offering extra top-ups over those offered by the rest of the UK. Providing affordable credit and savings is an important part of the Welsh financial inclusion strategy. Progressive top-ups add to this by providing extra help for those with problems in building a modest financial cushion. The top-ups were admittedly modest. However, these extra endowments were constrained by the Welsh government's budget and its limited capacity to raise revenue. Nevertheless, the Welsh government was different from those of the rest of the UK as it sought to make progressive universalism a much more important part of the CTF.

Progressive universalism was particularly important for the Welsh government (Morgan, 2006; Drakeford, 2007; Williams and Mooney, 2008; Chaney, 2009). First Minister of Wales Rhodri Morgan (2006) gave a speech in 2006 in which he set out the principles that should define a Welsh recipe for 21st-century socialism. Part of this involved aligning 'Labour in Wales with what is sometimes known as progressive universalism – a policy approach in which the benefits of universal services are retained, but where extra resources and policy attention is paid to those whose needs are greatest' (Morgan, 2006: 4). Hatherley (2011) notes that the Government of Wales Act 2006 contains a statutory duty unique to the UK requiring equality of opportunity for all services provided by the Welsh government (Government of Wales Act, 2006). She argues that this model of social justice implies a commitment to progressive universalism as it means that equality of opportunity will only prevail if access to services is open to all, with extra help being given to those most in need.

A Welsh addition to the CTF matched this rhetoric on progressive universalism. 'Taking everyone into account' (Welsh Government, 2009b: 50) declares that the 'Welsh Assembly Government aims to provide a Welsh premium to the CTF of all eligible children living in Wales from Autumn 2009. These eligible children will receive an additional £50, with those from low income families receiving an additional £50.' Mooney and Williams (2006) argue that devolved institutions often use social policy to build national identity. Welsh top-ups to the CTF seem a prime example of this as they were dubbed the CTF Cymru (Lewis, 2010a). The Welsh government promised to pay £50 extra in 2009/10 to all eligible children born between 1 September 2002 and 31 August 2003, with a further £50 for children from low-income households. Funding was also promised in 2010/11 for children born between 1 September 2003 and 31 August 2004 (Welsh Government, 2008). On 1 July 2009, the Welsh government stated that the first families would receive the Welsh top-ups, or CTF Cymru, in September 2009.

The Welsh government also made top-ups available to specific groups. It reimbursed local authorities for CTF payments of £50 per year per child for children in local authority care. In 2008, the Welsh government announced that it would raise this to £100 per year per child and also administer a UK scheme to pay £100 a year into the CTFs of children in care. This meant that the Welsh government reimbursed local authorities for £200 per year for children in care for more than one year since 1 April 2007, compared with the £100 top-up per year per child that the UK government provided for similar children in the rest of the UK (Welsh Government, 2008).

Constraints

The preceding discussion suggests that the Welsh government used progressive universalism to shape the CTF in different ways. The aforementioned steps should be set against the constraints that the Welsh government faces from the centre. The centre imposes constraints from both ideology and policy on the capacity of the Welsh government to pursue progressive universalism in one country. Mooney and Williams (2006) argue that efforts by the Welsh government to forge a distinct national identity are often constrained by a neoliberal agenda from the centre. They contend that, in practice, Welsh and Scottish social policy often modifies or adapts neoliberal approaches. Financialisation imposed constraints on the Welsh government insofar as it framed debates about assets in particular ways. Added to this were constraints from the austerity measures imposed by the UK government. Welsh politicians could not find the resources to continue the progressive universal payments into the CTF once they had been stopped by the Conservative–Liberal Democrat Coalition government. In a statement on 3 December 2010, the Deputy Minister for Children Huw Lewis (2010b: 2) wrote:

> In light of the UK Government's decision we have worked hard to find a way of continuing the CTF Cymru top-up and I have had a number of discussions with CTF providers to explore options. However, after much consideration it has become clear that it would not be feasible and I am very disappointed that as a consequence the CTF Cymru scheme will have to be wound up.

The politics of the Welsh government and the specific policy challenges facing Wales probably help explain why the Welsh government adapted asset-based welfare. A commitment to equality is built into the fabric of the Welsh government (Chaney, 2004, 2009; Drakeford, 2007). The Government of Wales Act 1998 contains a duty to promote equality of opportunity for all functions of government (Government of Wales Act, 1998). The Government of Wales Act 2006 extends this duty to cover Welsh Assembly ministers. Social justice has been an important part of the Welsh government's agenda since the first Assembly elections in 1999. Rhodri Morgan (2002: 7), who was the Labour First Minister between 2000 and 2009, stated in a speech at the National Centre for Public Policy in Swansea that 'I should make clear that my intention, ever since becoming First Minister, and looking ahead, is to lead a government of social justice, in which everything we do makes a maximum contribution to that end'. He presented this as part of 'clear red water' between the Welsh government and the Westminster Parliament (Morgan, 2002; Drakeford, 2005).

Financial inclusion

The Welsh government placed asset-based welfare within efforts to support financial inclusion. The Welsh government was not unique in its concern with financial inclusion (HM Treasury, 2004; Scottish Executive, 2005). The Welsh government was different insofar as its financial inclusion policy paid explicit attention to asset-based welfare. For example, Labour published a financial inclusion strategy in 2004 and established an independent Financial Inclusion Taskforce in 2005 to advise the Westminster government on policy. The Financial Inclusion Taskforce's homepage notes that it was charged to advise on access to affordable credit, banking and free face-to-face money advice. This strategy did not cover explicit attention to helping people build assets or savings, though later work by the Financial Inclusion Taskforce (2011) did cover saving.

In contrast, the Welsh government's financial inclusion policy had a much greater role for asset-based welfare. This embedded the CTF within its financial inclusion policy. In 2009, the Welsh government published an overall strategy for financial inclusion called 'Taking everyone into account' (Welsh Government, 2009b). This document highlights the critical role that low income plays in financial exclusion (Welsh Government, 2009b: 10). This explicitly sets the financial inclusion policy as focusing on the challenges facing those on low incomes. 'Taking everyone into account' (Welsh Government, 2009b) has five themes in its financial inclusion strategy, namely: access to mainstream financial services; providing affordable credit and savings; improving access to debt advice; boosting financial capability; and maximising income.

Credit unions

Asset-based welfare fell largely within the second strand of boosting affordable credit and savings. Part of this emphasised using credit unions to deliver CTFs (Welsh Government, 2009b). Credit unions are mutual financial institutions that are owned and run by their members. They do not make dividend payments to external shareholders. Credit unions have attracted interest within the general social policy community as one of the ways to reach out to low-income communities who have traditionally faced barriers in accessing financial services. Credit unions are thought to provide a more welcoming environment for low-income people than do mainstream banks. People are likely to feel more confident in dealing with an organisation in which they have an ownership stake. Conversely, financial bodies are less likely to ignore or neglect those people who have ownership rights in the organisation (McKillop and Wilson, 2008; Gregory and Drakeford, 2011; Morgan and Price, 2011). Credit unions often have to deposit their funds in banks, though many choose to deposit in the Co-operative Bank, which has an ethical investment policy. McKillop et al (2011) note that credit unions differ from the rest of the banking sector in not having access to interbank markets. This means the rates they charge on loans are not shaped by money markets (and these are capped at 2 per cent per month). McKillop et al (2011: 42) argue that the features of credit unions mean that they are not involved in the worst problems of financial markets:

> Credit unions are structured around a well-defined membership; they are not subject to shareholders' profit

expectations; and by legislation cannot provide high-risk structured financial products. For these reasons credit unions can be expected to be insulated from the worst excesses of the turmoil in financial markets, although any general economic downturn will impact equally on credit unions.

Although there is interest in credit unions within wider UK financial inclusion policy, the Welsh government is distinct in that it made it an explicit aim of policy to use asset-based welfare to increase the membership of credit unions. Gregory and Drakeford (2011) note that credit unions were not originally allowed to take CTF accounts. The Welsh government pressed for change:

> When the CTF was launched, in September 2005, credit unions were not among the list of financial institutions where deposits could be made. ... The Welsh Assembly Government provided funding to support a demonstration project, aimed at showing how credit unions could increase their shares and membership through attracting CTF deposits. (Gregory and Drakeford, 2011: 122)

The Welsh government set a target of increasing the number of credit unions being able to offer CTF accounts from three to 18 by June 2009, which would represent 60 per cent of credit unions in Wales. The Welsh government provided £350,000 to help achieve this target, and the goal was achieved by May 2009. Welsh credit unions comprised 25 per cent of CTF providers in the UK (Welsh Government, 2009a). In 2018, there were around 79,000 members of credit unions in Wales, compared with roughly 841,000 members of credit unions in England (Bank of England, 2019).

Automatic enrolment into a workplace pension in the UK

Chapter 2 discussed behavioural economics and mentioned the automatic enrolment into a workplace pension. This section looks more closely at how this idea has been implemented in the UK. AE in the UK is interesting as it is cited as a possible way that occupational pensions might be advancing financialisation in Europe (Natali, 2018).

UK AE was introduced alongside wider reforms to UK pensions (Thurley, 2019). One important change was the introduction of the single-tier pension after 6 April 2016. The value of the single-tier pension is about the basic level of means-tested support (at least

£151.25 per week in 2015/16). The value of the state pension in 2019–20 is £168.60 per week (Gov.UK, 2019). The single-tier pension was aimed at simplifying the system of pension provision and boosting further saving. The Department for Work and Pensions (2013a: 54) notes that people 'will receive the flat rate single-tier payment as a foundation on which to save, and will be further encouraged and supported to save into a workplace pension scheme through automatic enrolment'.

AE was introduced from October 2012, with the largest employers introducing AE first. Employers with 250 or more workers in their largest pay-as-you-earn system were staged between October 2012 and February 2014. Employers with 50 to 249 employees were then staged between 1 April 2014 and 1 April 2015. Employers with fewer than 50 employees were staged between 1 June 2015 and 1 April 2017 (Pensions Regulator, 2014).

UK AE is aimed broadly at low to moderate earners. The UK government uses replacement rates to model whether or not people have adequate income in retirement. The replacement rate is income in retirement as a percentage of income in work. In the UK government approach, pre-retirement income is defined as gross income calculated before deductions for tax and pension contributions, and is the average of positive earnings from age 50 to the state pension age. Retirement income is state and private pension income and is the average gross income from the state pension age onwards (Department for Work and Pensions, 2013b). The ideal replacement rate is not necessarily 100 per cent as people may have fewer income needs once retired (for example, mortgages may be paid off). Target replacement rates are aimed at ensuring that people have a similar standard of living before and after retirement. The UK government claims that target replacement rates vary from 80 per cent for very low earners to 50 per cent for high earners (Department for Work and Pensions, 2013b). UK government analysis suggests the single-tier pension combined with saving in AE at the default rate should provide 93 per cent of very low earners with their target replacement rate. High earners are thought to have adequate pension provision through private pensions. AE is targeted at low to moderate earners as these people are thought to face a shortfall in their replacement rate. A specific target group for government policy are those people who were not saving in a pension scheme when AE was introduced or those people who were members of a scheme where the employer contributed less than 3 per cent of a person's salary and this employer contribution was not into a defined benefit scheme (Department for Work and Pensions, 2013b, 2015a).

Two conditions define eligibility for AE: first, people need to be aged 22 years old or over but below the state retirement age; and, second, people need to earn within a particular income range. The trigger for AE is set as the threshold for paying income tax. This means that the earnings trigger for AE was £10,000 per year in 2014–15. This earnings trigger has stayed the same through to 2019–20. The thresholds for qualifying earnings define the income range from which pension contributions can be made. The lower threshold for qualifying earnings is at the National Insurance Contributions primary threshold. The minimum level for qualifying earnings was £5,772 per year in 2014–15 and £6,316 per year in 2019–20. The upper limit for qualifying earnings is set at the National Insurance Contributions upper earnings threshold. This was £41,865 per year in 2014–15 and £50,000 per year in 2019–20 (Pensions Regulator, 2019).

Under AE, there is a minimum 8 per cent contribution from a person's qualifying earnings into retirement savings in a defined contribution scheme. Employers have to contribute at least 3 per cent of this 8 per cent total contribution rate. The full default rate was introduced gradually and took full effect from April 2019. Thus, there was a rising default rate under AE. Up to 30 September 2017, there is a minimum total contribution rate of 2 per cent (with employers contributing at least 1 per cent). From 1 April 2018, the minimum total contribution rate rose to 5 per cent (with a minimum employer contribution of 2 per cent). The 8 per cent total contribution rate applied from 1 April 2019 (HM Treasury, 2015b).

Employees have to opt out through an opt-out notice. They have up to one calendar month to opt out once they are enrolled in a scheme if they wish to receive a full refund of their contributions. If people opt out later, then their payments may stay in the pension until they retire. AE policy requires that employers issue and collect opt-out notices. This policy spells out the minimum content of these notices. The notice must inform the employee that the employer cannot ask or force the employee to opt out, that people will be re-enrolled after about three years, and that if they change jobs, the person will be reassessed for AE (Pensions Regulator, 2017).

Employers are allowed to adapt any existing occupational pension scheme to meet the requirements for AE (though some commentators worry this might lead to a levelling down of existing pension provision (Van de Ven, 2012)). These requirements vary depending on the type of existing pension (such as defined contribution, defined benefit or a hybrid scheme) (Department for Work and Pensions, 2014a). The government has also set up a pension provider in case an employer does not set up their own scheme. This is called the National Employment Savings Trust (NEST). NEST is set up as a public benefit company. Any surplus is reinvested in the company and is not paid as dividend payments to shareholders (National Employment Savings Trust Corporation, 2015).

Qualitative research

Feldman (2018) argues that studying the reactions of users is important for revealing the barriers that low-income people may face in saving. The rest of this chapter responds to this call by presenting original qualitative research into public attitudes towards automatic enrolment into a workplace pension. However, there is surprisingly little data on public attitudes to pension reforms in general, as well as to AE in particular (Foster, 2012; MacLeod et al, 2012; Jaime-Castillo, 2013; Inland Revenue, 2015). So far, three countries have introduced AE at a national level, that is, the UK, Italy and New Zealand (Collard and Moore, 2010; Rinaldi, 2011; Collard, 2013). The Italian government introduced AE in 2007 as part of its reforms of its severance pay system called Trattamento di Fine Rapporto (Fornero and Monticone, 2011; Rinaldi, 2011). New Zealand introduced KiwiSaver in 2007, which automatically enrols people into a special savings scheme when they start a new job (though others, including children, can opt in to KiwiSaver) (Inland Revenue, 2012, 2015). However, limited research exists on why people do or do not opt out of AE in either the Italian or New Zealand schemes (Rinaldi, 2011; Fornero and Monticone, 2011; Inland Revenue, 2012, 2015). The small work that has been done on opt-outs in New Zealand suggests that lack of affordability is the most common reason for opting out of KiwiSaver (Inland Revenue, 2015).

Qualitative methods allow a high degree of sensitivity to the views of participants (Bloor et al, 2000; Barbour, 2007; Stewart et al, 2007). Qualitative methods were well suited for this study as they allowed the research to investigate a range of possible reasons for why people did or did not opt out of AE. This probing was important given that people may have given little thought to not opting out of the pension. These methods were also important for discovering issues that were raised by the participants themselves. This evidence gathering was particularly significant as there was little prior data on public attitudes to AE.

Focus groups were used in this study. Discussion within the focus groups allowed a range of views to be explored and highlighted common themes among participants. Recommended practices for focus groups were used in this research. For example, the moderator for each group facilitated discussion among all members of the group and allowed reflection once common themes were identified (Bloor et al, 2000; Barbour, 2007; Stewart et al, 2007).

A market research company was used to recruit participants for the focus groups. This used standard market research filters, such as not using people who had taken part in a similar project in the recent past. People were recruited on the basis of informed consent and a £30 payment was made to cover travel expenses and as a reward for taking part in the study. People were informed about the aim and purpose of this project at the start of each focus group. Permission was sought and granted for the focus groups to be audiotaped and transcribed. The group discussions lasted about one hour each.

Greater London was chosen as a location to conduct this research as there was a broad range of large employers that had already introduced AE. The focus groups were convened in April and early June 2014 (tax year 2014–15). During the recruitment process, a maximum limit of eight people was set on the membership of each focus group. This number was picked as this allowed discussion to occur in each group. Overall, 44 people took part in this study. The numbers involved in this study are comparable to similar qualitative research elsewhere (Opinion Leader Research, 2006; GfK NOP Social Research, 2010).

The age bands used in the Department for Work and Pensions (2013c, 2014b, 2014c, 2015b) studies were also used here, namely, people in their 20s/30s, 40s and 50s. Studying opt-outs and non-opt-outs in each of the age cohorts meant that the research was interested in six groups of the eligible population for AE. Three of the groups were made up of opt-outs among the three age cohorts, namely, people in their 20s/30s, 40s and 50s. Three of the other groups were made up of people who had not opted out. Each of these non-opt-out groups contained a mix of employees. Some of these people were not members of a workplace pension before AE was introduced. They form a specific target group for this policy. Research has shown that around two thirds of employers have increased their total pension contributions since the introduction of AE (Department for Work and Pensions, 2014d; Clarke et al, 2018). The introduction of AE might change the reasons why existing members belong to a scheme. To explore this possibility, the groups of non-opt-outs also included employees who were members of a workplace pension once AE was introduced.

An extra seventh group of opt-outs of people in their 20s/30s was also convened as there were fewer people in the original 20s/30s opt-out group than the other groups. Thus, there were seven groups in total in this research.

The eligible population meant participants were aged between 22 years of age and the state retirement age. People also needed to earn an income between the trigger for AE and the upper limit for qualifying earnings. For 2014–15, this meant people earning between £10,000 and £41,865. To allow the research to study the impact of gender on opt-outs, roughly equal numbers of men and women were convened in each focus group.

Two main questions were asked in the focus groups. First, how much do people know about AE? Examining awareness of AE was important for assessing the extent to which people were making informed decisions about whether or not to opt out of AE. Lack of awareness of pensions is a relevant issue in the UK. Research suggests low public knowledge of state pensions in the UK (Clery et al, 2009; MacLeod et al, 2012). It was not possible in the time available to explore all aspects of the different types of scheme. Instead, the research focused on awareness of the requirements for defined contribution schemes. This was because evidence suggested that defined contribution schemes were the most common type of scheme offered by private sector employers for new enrolees (Department for Work and Pensions, 2014d).

The second set of questions asked people the reasons for opting out or not opting out. The discussion of non-opt-outs adds to previous Department for Work and Pensions research.

The quotations used in the following are illustrative of the main themes that arose in the discussions. Qualitative research of the type reported here allows for an intermediate level of generalisation between universal generalisation and no generalisation at all (Foster, 2012; Payne and Williams, 2005). Foster (2012) remarks that such intermediate generalisation is often unavoidable in qualitative research.

Results

Are people aware of AE?

The focus groups echoed findings from earlier research that suggested poor knowledge of pensions (Clery et al, 2009; MacLeod et al, 2012). Most people did not know the starting age for AE. Common responses were 16 or 18 years old, which was cited because they were the school leaving age or the age of majority. People tended to guess that the upper age range was the state retirement age. Very few participants mentioned an income band for AE.

There was uncertainty about which employers were required to provide AE. A common response was that AE might only apply to large or medium-sized employers. Participants often suggested that smaller employers would be excluded. These responses were perhaps unsurprising given that large employers were in the first wave of employers providing AE and many participants belonged to large employers and so drew on their own experience.

There was patchy knowledge across the focus groups of the default rate for AE (and little sense of the tax advantages of pensions). Among those who did not opt out, there was some knowledge that the minimum employer contribution was 1 per cent when AE was first introduced. However, across all groups, there was little sense that the default savings rate would eventually rise to 8 per cent. Furthermore, people did not have much idea of why 8 per cent was picked as the default savings rate: "Maybe it is the Chancellor's lucky number" (50s, opt-out, female). Nearly all participants were aware that they were able to opt out from AE. The actual opting-out process was usually described as very easy. Participants said that they had been informed about this by their human resources department and that people were able to opt out easily, for example, through email.

The focus groups also explored knowledge of the single-tier pension. The aim was to see whether the single-tier pension had shaped decisions of whether or not to opt out of a workplace pension. There was poor knowledge of the single-tier pension and so the single-tier pension did not impact on decisions about whether or not to opt out.

Why do people not opt out?

To isolate the UK government's target group for this policy, participants were asked whether or not they were a member of a pension scheme when AE was introduced. Members of the UK government's target group for AE tended to be concentrated in the 20s/30s or 40s age cohorts.

Among those in the target group, status quo bias seemed to be important for their decision not to opt out:

> 'When I came out of university, I had my student loan to pay, so at the time I felt I need to focus on repaying that first. Obviously, that was coming directly out of my salary and then I was just lazy, so I appreciate the fact that this opting-in scheme to get things to a certain level, I need to do, I need to do it, I just never got around to it. Then, obviously, through work, we got notification that we would

automatically opted in. I just thought, "Oh, you have saved me a job."' (20s/30s, non-opt-out, female)

An important reason behind the power of suggestion for the target group was that AE had simplified the decision about how to be a member of a workplace pension: "I didn't know how to get involved in a pension and now it is done automatically and the amount that is going out every month, I am not really missing it too much" (20s/30s, non-opt-out, male). A lack of appropriate information or advice seemed to be a more significant reason behind the power of suggestion: "Who is going to give individual, real, true independent advice? I don't know; that would concern me. You might think you are getting independent advice and it is not, so how will I know which one to go for?" (50s, non-opt-out, female). There was less engagement with AE among participants who were already a member of a pension scheme when AE was introduced. One issue among these people was that there was little sense of whether their pension scheme had changed since AE. Those people who were members of a defined contribution scheme could not say whether or not their total contribution rate had changed since AE.

Why do people opt out?

Previous Department for Work and Pensions (2014b, 2014c, 2015b) research highlights that lack of affordability or the presence of preferable alternatives to pensions are key reasons that people opt out of AE. The research in the focus groups for this chapter confirmed these earlier findings. Lack of affordability was cited as a prime reason for opting out, particularly, though not exclusively, for younger cohorts in their 20s/30s or 40s.

There was little evidence from the groups that employers had placed (illegal) pressure on women to opt out. However, women were more likely than men in all opt-out groups to cite lack of affordability as a reason for opting out. This tendency was consistent with a gender pay and pension gap in the UK. Tighter financial constraints on women meant that female participants were more likely to cite affordability as a reason for opting out:

'I'm a teacher, so you have to have a pension. About six years ago, I had my son, and my partner and I split up, so I couldn't afford to have my pension, and my pension is ridiculous when it comes out, it's about, well, at that time, it was about £300, £400. I just couldn't afford to and then when this new scheme came in, they put me back in it and then I had to re-opt back out.' (20s/30s, opt-out, female)

Men were more likely than women to mention the presence of more financially attractive alternatives to a pension as a reason for opting out.

Another difference between men and women was over the role that childcare played in decisions to opt out. This is consistent with other research which suggests that the financial costs of raising children is felt more strongly by women than by men (Ginn and Arber, 2002). None of the male opt-outs cited childcare as a reason for opting out. However, a couple of women in the group of opt-outs aged in the 20s/30s mentioned childcare as their main reason for opting out. For these participants, the childcare costs were high because the children were of pre-school age. These responses also underline how people face competing cost pressures at different points in their life and so pension saving may not always be a priority: "Mine [the reason for opting out] was childcare because it costs one, to have a child in full-time childcare costs £1,200 a month" (20s/30s, opt-out, female).

Discussion

There is good evidence that AE boosts the membership of workplace pensions. This increases the involvement in the financial system and so contributes to financial inclusion. However, AE also has important limitations and this reveals issues with financial inclusion. Although AE increases the membership of a workplace pension, it may nevertheless favour certain parts of the population. This means that financial inclusion policies can still, paradoxically, exclude certain groups from participation in the financial system.

The current design of AE arguably systematically favours men over women. The policy may reinforce rather than reduce gender inequality in pensions. Grady (2015) argues that the UK pension system is based on 'hetero-patriarchal' assumptions. This means that the pension system implicitly assumes that the typical worker is a full-time male worker with a full contributions record. She says that this ignores the inferior status of women in the labour market. Data from the European Union show that the average gross hourly earnings of women were about 16 per cent less than men across the European Union in 2017. In the UK, this gender pay gap was about 20.8 per cent. Women earn less than men because they do most of the unpaid care in society and often have to work part-time to perform these caring duties (Dessimirova and

Bustamante, 2019). For example, European data highlight that around one third of women (31.7 per cent) across the European Union in 2018 report that caring responsibilities were the main reason for not being a member of the labour force, compared with 4.6 per cent of men (Eurostat, 2019).

European Union data show that a gender pension gap outstripped a gender pay gap across the European Union. For pensioners aged 65–79 years, women's pensions were about 35.7 per cent lower than those of men in 2017. The gender pension gap in the UK was 36.2 per cent (Dessimirova and Bustamante, 2019). Grady (2015) claims that apparently gender-blind reforms such as AE leave this underlying gender inequality untouched. Women can expect fewer benefits than men in AE because lower earnings limit their possible contributions. Furthermore, women are more likely than men to be excluded from AE because of low earnings. Thurley (2019) reports that government estimates show that an earnings trigger of £10,000 per year for 2014–15 means that 69 per cent of the excluded are women. Van de Ven (2012) states that AE will have a disproportionate impact on employer costs in low-pay industries as many of these employers have not provided pensions previously. He says that employers might offset AE by cutting wages and this has gender implications because just under half of all women work in low-pay industries, compared to under 30 per cent of men. Ginn and MacIntyre (2013) suggest that employers might put (illegal) pressure on employees, especially women, to opt out in order to avoid paying employer AE contributions.

The Department for Work and Pensions (2015b) says that opt-out rates were 7 per cent for workers aged under 30, 9 per cent for those aged between 30 and 49, and 23 per cent for those aged 50 or over. Clarke et al (2018) argue that the opt-out rate from AE in 2016–17 was about 9 per cent of employees who were automatically enrolled and that this rate had not changed much since 2015. Lack of affordability or other provisions for retirement were cited in general as the main reasons for opting out. Workers aged 50 or over also mentioned the relatively short time they would spend in AE as a key reason for opting out. The limited time in AE meant these workers expected that their personal contributions would only yield poor returns. One strand of further work might explore the different pressures that face women when opting out, for example, looking at the role that childcare costs play in decisions to opt out. Another strand of research might focus on those women who are enrolled in a workplace pension. Further studies might look at whether it is possible to design AE to recognise the unpaid care contributions made by women (through carers' credits in AE) in order to reduce the gender pension gap (Ginn and MacIntyre, 2013).

Another issue with AE is that people may display little activity once they are enrolled in a workplace pension. The status quo bias which means that people do not opt out of a pension may also mean that people show little activity once they are in a scheme. Of course, certain further behavioural nudges might be used to address this issue, for example, by having a default savings rate. However, it may be difficult to pick a default savings rate that guarantees an adequate replacement rate for all parts of the population. Certain groups may have to save beyond a default savings rate to have an adequate replacement rate.

There may be a need to support further engagement but this may imply going beyond behavioural nudges. Providing information or guidance alongside AE is one way of trying to achieve this. Dolan et al (2010) argue that people are heavily influenced by the source or 'messenger' of information. The government and employers might be likely channels for such information. It is also important to distinguish between advice and guidance in the provision of information. HM Treasury and the Financial Conduct Authority in the UK recently conducted a financial advice market review. This review defines advice as information that contains a personal recommendation for individuals (such as over their specific contribution rate). Guidance is used to refer to more general information that does not involve a personal recommendation for individuals (HM Treasury and FCA, 2016). One issue to study is therefore the proper mix between advice and guidance in the provision of information. There is no consensus as yet, though, about the proper balance of advice and guidance or the likely impact of financial education on financial decisions (Willis, 2008; Lusardi and Mitchell, 2011).

Conclusion

This chapter has examined financial inclusion savings policies. It has looked particularly at the CTF as well as the automatic enrolment into a workplace pension. These examples are important as they are innovative examples of savings policies that have prompted much international interest. This chapter has suggested that the policies may be designed in different ways, and that not all versions of the policies are aimed at turning people into investor-subjects. Features such as progressive universalism and the use of credit unions to deliver the CTF point to different ways of designing this policy. The chapter has also claimed that important issues remain to be addressed with the automatic enrolment into a workplace pension. One key issue here is the need to address a gender inequality within pensions. Chapter 4 builds on some of the arguments in this chapter by highlighting the links that exist between financial markets and other markets. Chapter 4 studies housing as this has a strong linkage with the financial system and sets financial inclusion in a wider context.

4

The case of housing

Introduction

An investor-subject critique is at the heart of criticisms of financial inclusion. This critique is driven by the idea that people are shifted from the security of the welfare state to the insecurity of financial markets. This chapter studies the case of housing. It does this because housing is arguably one of the most important investments made by investor-subjects and this case highlights the connections that exist between the financial system and other parts of the economy. Hofman and Aalbers (2019: 91; see also Jordà et al, 2014) comment that the:

> alleged dominance of finance is in many ways interdependent with real estate. For example: real estate has become the single largest form of collateral that banks provide credit on. Between 1870 and 2010, the share of mortgage loans in banks' total lending portfolios doubled from 30 to 60 per cent in a group of 17 OECD countries including the US, Canada, Australia, Japan, the UK and 12 other European states. ... Finance may dominate the economy, but real estate finance dominates banking.

Smith (2008) underlines the connection between housing and the financial system. Drawing on two qualitative studies done in the UK, she explores the conceptual links between housing, home and finance. Smith (2008) argues that 'home' has a variety of meanings. In the English-speaking world, she claims that the notion of home has become closely bound up with the idea of an investment. This means that the homeowner is seen to be an investor rather than a property-owning citizen. Smith (2008) argues that these home investors need access to mortgage markets to be able to make investments and so housing is bound up with financial markets. She writes that in places such as the US and UK:

> homeowning (or homebuying, at least) is the dominant housing style, and it takes a particular form: it is funded,

insured, and to an extent marketed and managed, by a
stream of financial services which link households' cash
economy (their behaviours around savings, spending and
debt) into the world of international finance. (Smith,
2008: 520)

Home-ownership is thought to provide security in retirement as well as
a basis for consumer spending. Housing is itself a consumption good and
so people can consume the services provided by housing in retirement
(for example, consuming shelter and warmth). Home-ownership can
also be used to provide people with a retirement income through
equity release schemes (Smith, 2008; Lowe, 2012). Significant annual
house price rises allow people to consume beyond their income from
paid work (for example, homeowners may use housing as a way to get
credit) (Crouch, 2008; Watson, 2008).

Research suggests that the stress on home-ownership fuels two trends
in housing markets. The first is an emphasis on 'borrowing to invest'.
Housing is often the most expensive purchase that people will make
in their lives and people will usually have to borrow on mortgage
markets to be able to buy a house. Borrowing is therefore a key part
of the investor-subject approach. A paradox is that an approach aimed
at encouraging home-ownership licenses a growth in personal debt.

The second trend in housing markets is the easy availability of credit.
If people are to borrow to buy housing, then there should be easy access
to credit. Governments therefore relaxed the constraints on lending
by financial companies. In places such as the US and UK, there was
light-touch regulation of financial institutions. This led to the growth
of lending to low-income people on the 'sub-prime' market (Langley,
2008; Montgomerie, 2008; Montgomerie and Büdenbender, 2015).

A link is made here between housing and access to credit markets.
This highlights that it is important to see financial inclusion alongside
other policy agendas. This connection between the financial system and
housing matters because of its impacts on the global economy (Watson,
2008, 2009, 2010; Toussaint and Elsinga, 2009; Doling and Ronald,
2010b; Lowe et al, 2011; Ronald and Doling, 2012; Montgomerie
and Büdenbender, 2015; Stebbing and Spies-Butcher, 2016; Walks,
2016; Lennartz and Ronald, 2017; Ronald et al, 2017). For example,
the collapse of a house price bubble in the 'sub-prime' housing market
in the US and UK is often seen as one of the triggers of the 2007–08
banking and financial crisis (Watson, 2008, 2009, 2010; Lowe et al,
2011; Montgomerie and Büdenbender, 2015).

This chapter is organised as follows. The first part outlines privatised Keynesianism as this is an influential political-economy account of the link between the financial system and housing. The second section notes that the emphasis on home-ownership is often seen as part of asset-based welfare but claims that it is important to distinguish the assets discussed in Chapter 3 from housing. The third section suggests that it is important to develop a new model of housing to help form an alternative to an investor-subject approach. It argues that the taxation of housing and creating new forms of home-ownership are important for striking a new agenda. The fourth part applies this new agenda to one of the key challenges facing housing, that is, the struggle that millennials face in buying a home.

Privatised Keynesianism

Recent political economy draws attention to 'privatised Keynesianism' as an unacknowledged policy regime after the end of the Second World War (Crouch, 2009; Watson, 2010; Hofman and Aalbers, 2019; Wijburg, 2019). Wijburg (2019: 146) comments that 'Privatised Keynesianism has become widely known as the unacknowledged but neoliberal successor of Keynesianism-Fordism: a policy regime in which households, rather than the state, take up credit to stimulate the economy.'

Conventional wisdom suggests that Keynesianism and neoliberalism became the two dominant policy regimes after the end of the Second World War. Keynesianism drew from the economic ideas of John Maynard Keynes and is thought to have been the main influence on economic policy from 1945 to the 1970s. The core of Keynesianism is that governments should use tax and spending to manage demand in an economy. If overall demand is low in the economy, then this leads to unemployment. A key insight of Keynesian economics is that public borrowing can be used to stimulate the economy in a recession. In particular, public borrowing can be used to pay for a programme of public spending such as building roads. Government spending then has a 'multiplier effect' as it stimulates private spending. This increases overall demand in an economy that feeds through into higher employment. Wijburg (2019) mentions Fordism alongside Keynesianism. Fordism concerns the mass production of standard goods. Keynesianism was aimed at supporting mass production as well as mass consumption. If the economy is at full employment and there is rising inflation, then governments could intervene to stabilise the economy by raising taxes and perhaps reducing public spending. Demand will drop and the inflationary pressures would subside.

Keynesian demand management seemed to work well until the 1970s, after which time it seemed to break down. Government spending did not seem able to reduce unemployment and coexisted with high inflation in economies such as the UK. The apparent failure of Keynesian demand management sparked a challenge from supporters of free markets. Theorists such as Milton Friedman and Friedrich von Hayek argued in favour of free markets and a small state. For these thinkers, rather than trying to manage demand, the key task of government is to reform the supply side by encouraging competition and extending the reach of free markets. Politicians such as President Ronald Reagan in the US and Prime Minister Margaret Thatcher in the UK formed a willing audience for these free market ideas. This seemed to then usher in the dominance of neoliberal ideology and policy.

Of course, the reality is more complex than the preceding sketch suggests. Scholars have questioned whether there was genuine consensus over Keynesian social democracy at the end of the Second World War. It is also possible that government intervention in the economy was more a legacy of the growth in the size of the state during the Second World War than driven by Keynes's ideas.

Debates also exist about the nature of neoliberalism. Politicians such as Reagan and Thatcher were arguably more pragmatic than neoliberal ideology would suggest. Thatcher found it difficult to roll back the frontiers of the state. Crouch (2008, 2009) claims that the content of the neoliberal policy regime has commonly been misunderstood. He says that the main change that occurred in the 1970s was a shift in emphasis from public to private debt as the basis for economic growth. The second policy regime 'was not, as often been thought, a neo-liberal turn to pure markets, but a system of markets alongside extensive housing and other debt among low- and medium-income people linked to unregulated derivative markets. It was a form of privatised Keynesianism' (Crouch, 2009: 382).

Borrowing to spend to stimulate the economy in a recession is important for Keynesian thought. Privatising Keynesianism means shifting the debt from the public to the private sector. Crouch (2008, 2009) suggests that the main way that governments sought to expand private debt was by encouraging the growth of mortgage debt. Crouch (2008: 476) says that:

> Under original Keynesianism it was governments that took
> on debt to stimulate the economy. Under the privatised

form individuals, particularly poor ones, took on that role by incurring debt on the market. The main motors were the near constant rise in the value of owner-occupied houses and apartments alongside an extraordinary growth in markets in risk.

Thus, the government stressed the importance of home-ownership among the population and wanted to improve access to mortgage lending. Indeed, scholars refer to 'house price Keynesianism' to underline the significance of housing for privatised Keynesianism (Watson, 2010; Wijburg, 2019).

One development since the financial crisis of 2008–09 has been a drop in home-ownership in places such as the UK. This has meant that the content of house price Keynesianism has changed since the financial crisis. As Ronald, Lennartz and Kadi (2017: 185, emphasis in original) claim: 'While the GFC [Great Financial Crisis] helped undermine the *home ownership* base of asset-based welfare, the crisis actually helped refine the role of *housing property* in social, economic and welfare relations.'

One result of this is that more attention is paid to private landlordism as part of house price Keynesianism. Ronald, Lennartz and Kadi (2017: 183) write that the 'new landlordism has been shaped by the "investor subject" of asset-based welfare'. Soaita et al (2017) extend this discussion by outlining findings from a qualitative research project on landlords' motives for the private rental sector as an asset strategy. Their results show that there are different motives for landlordism and these motives vary depending on the type of landlord. For example, some landlords use the private rental sector to provide immediate income, while others see it as a source of income for the future through capital gains. In particular, landlords with small portfolios may see property as a key way of paying for retirement.

Wijburg (2019) argues that it is important to expand the concept of house price Keynesianism to include private landlordism. He claims that 'Far more than a policy regime that merely promotes mortgaged home ownership, privatised Keynesianism is a flexible regime of accumulation, which potentially links different kinds of households to household debt, including private landlords' (Wijburg, 2019: 144). He says that house price Keynesianism is often associated with those countries that have sought to expand home-ownership, such as the UK and US. Wijburg (2019) contends that this focus on home-ownership overlooks how countries such as France used state-backed credit to expand private landlordism and the private rental sector. This means that the relevance of house price Keynesianism goes beyond the Anglo-American sphere and applies to countries with much lower home-ownership rates, such as France.

Asset-based welfare and housing

Housing scholars argue that governments have used asset-based welfare to drive the growth in home-ownership (Watson, 2008, 2009, 2010; Toussaint and Elsinga, 2009; Doling and Ronald, 2010a, 2010b; Ronald and Doling, 2012; Lowe et al, 2011; Montgomerie and Büdenbender, 2015; Stebbing and Spies-Butcher, 2016; Walks, 2016; Wijburg, 2019). Wijburg (2019: 144) notes that:

> housing scholars have pointed out that the extensive growth of mortgage debt associated with this regime is often fiscally and financially encouraged by governments that seek to switch households from the public housing sector into the private sector. ... Therefore, privatised Keynesianism or 'house price Keynesianism' can also be perceived as a partially state-enhanced asset-based welfare regime in which households can compensate for reduced income and welfare by continually trading up the value of their housing assets.

Asset-based welfare was explored in Chapter 3 on financial inclusion and saving. Chapter 3 points to overlaps between savings and housing. Saving is usually done for a purpose rather than being a worthwhile activity in itself. One aim of long-term saving is to prepare for retirement. Another common aim of long-term saving is to save for a deposit on a home. Sherraden's (1991) IDAs, which pioneered much of asset-based welfare, have saving for a deposit on a home as one of the express aims of the account.

Asset-based welfare focuses mainly on small amounts of financial wealth (Gregory, 2016). However, this has prompted a criticism that asset-based welfare fails to recognise the dominant role that housing plays in the assets owned by large parts of the population (Watson, 2008, 2009, 2010; Toussaint and Elsinga, 2009; Doling and Ronald, 2010a, 2010b; Ronald and Doling, 2012; Lowe et al, 2011; Montgomerie and Büdenbender, 2015; Stebbing and Spies-Butcher, 2016; Walks, 2016; Lennartz and Ronald, 2017; Ronald et al, 2017; Soaita et al, 2017). Doling and Ronald (2010a: 165, emphasis in original) report that the '*asset* in asset-based welfare has frequently become *property or housing asset*'. They also illustrate that in the late 1990s and early 2000s, housing wealth formed between a third and a half of personal wealth in France, Germany, Italy and the UK (Doling and Ronald, 2010b). Official data from the Wealth and Assets Survey for 2014 to 2016 show that property is the single most important part of total wealth for the fourth to seventh decile (10 per cent slice) of the wealth distribution in Great Britain. For example, property forms around 44 per cent of total wealth for the sixth decile. For the poorest in society (first decile), physical wealth such as collectibles is the most important source of wealth. For the wealthiest (tenth decile), private pension wealth is the most important type of wealth. Other research on households with a head of household aged 55 years or over shows that housing is over 80 per cent of personal wealth in Greece, Italy and Spain (Lefebure et al, 2006).

An asset-based welfare approach that does not pay attention to housing will not fashion practical proposals on asset ownership that have the most impact on the lives of most people. Nevertheless, this section claims that asset-based welfare and housing refer to different things. Housing asset-based welfare is centrally concerned with investment in housing. An important strand of the asset effect is about *non-investment*. An important strand of policies such as Help to Save is about people building a modest financial buffer to protect themselves against relatively common shocks.

There is some recognition within the recent housing literature that asset-based welfare focuses on non-investment. Lennartz and Ronald (2017) present asset-based welfare as an alternative to social investment. They claim that asset-based welfare is aimed at providing people with the conventional protections supplied by the welfare state as this policy approach allows the welfare state to target particular types of spending aimed at social investment. Thus, asset-based welfare contributes to the reshaping rather than retrenchment of the welfare state: 'ABW [asset-based welfare] – and particularly the idea of bringing new households into the homeownership sector through early life debt accumulation – is basically a response to the (budgetary) strains when keeping old risk social policies in place' (Lennartz and Ronald, 2017: 213–14). Here, asset-based welfare is associated with conventional social protections offered by the welfare state, albeit of a different scope and nature.

Even where asset-based welfare is used for investment, this is usually for non-housing assets. IDAs are Sherraden's (1991) main policy idea. Housing is only one of the aims of IDAs, and arguably the least realistic of the suggested uses as the matched savings are more likely to be used for non-housing investments such as job-related training or starting a business. As noted in Chapter 3, Sherraden and his colleagues conducted an American Dream Demonstration project that reported results from pilots of IDAs. This research showed that the average net monthly deposit per participant was US$19.07 and people accumulated about US$700 a year in their IDAs (Schreiner et al, 2002). These savings are not enough to be used as a deposit on a home.

Asset-based welfare and housing also differ over the role of income. Sherraden's (1991) argument is that assets are fundamentally different to income. Borrowing to invest is a key part of the investor-subject approach. Borrowing points to the importance of a flow of income (debt). In fact, housing asset-based welfare suggests that asset-based welfare contributed to a rise in general indebtedness in places such as the UK (Lowe et al, 2011). This growth in indebtedness leads to dependence on the lender rather than independence and so there is a fundamental difference between the investor-subject (whose name implies subjection or dependence) and the empowered individuals within asset-based welfare.

Recent contributions to housing also highlight how housing is used to provide people with flows of income to meet future welfare needs (Fox O'Mahony and Overton, 2015; Overton and Fox O'Mahony, 2017; Soaita and Searle, 2016; Soaita et al, 2017; Lennartz and Ronald, 2017; Ronald et al, 2017). Ronald, Lennartz and Kadi (2017) claim that home-ownership was the main focus of asset-based welfare prior to the financial crisis. They say that although there has been less emphasis on asset-based welfare policy after the financial crisis, housing remains important for addressing the welfare needs of households in a period dominated by austerity cuts to public spending. Lennartz and Ronald (2017) and Ronald, Lennartz and Kadi (2017) outline four ways that home-ownership can provide people with a flow of income. First, there is the imputed rent that can be associated with home-ownership. Second, there are equity release products that allow owners to access the equity stored in their property to create income (see also Fox O'Mahony and Overton, 2015; Overton and Fox O'Mahony, 2017). Third, people can raise money by downsizing from their property. Fourth, people can create a flow of money by renting out rooms or becoming private landlords by acquiring more property by leveraging their home (see also Soaita et al, 2017).

Developing a different model of housing

The discussion of privatised Keynesianism highlights that the investor-subject approach supports a particular view of housing. Developing a different model of housing may be important for breaking the hold of this investor-subject approach and recasting the relationship between the financial system and housing. This may also make it easier to fashion a better model of financial inclusion rather than a version that might lead to a house price bubble.

One way of trying to develop a different model of housing is to explore the potential of an egalitarian property-owning democracy. Meade (1964) used the term 'egalitarian property-owning democracy' to refer to an effort to spread wealth to create a more equal society (Meade, 1964; Rawls, 1971). The phrase 'property-owning democracy' originates on the Right. The Conservative politician Noel Skelton introduced the term 'property-owning democracy' during the 1920s and this has since been an important theme of Conservative politics (Skelton, 1924; Hogg, 1947; Ron, 2008). Skelton's aim in developing this concept was to protect the rights of property-holders from the growth in mass democracy (Skelton, 1924; Ron, 2008; Gregory, 2016). Property-owning democracy has probably been associated most closely with Prime Minister Margaret Thatcher's sale of council homes and privatising nationalised utilities such as gas and water during the 1980s (Gamble and Kelly, 1996; Ron, 2008; Lund, 2013).

The Centre-Left recognises that the sale of council houses is a species of property-owning democracy (Gamble and Kelly, 1996; Ackerman and Alstott, 1999). However, these theorists are critical of Thatcherism because they say that she did not seek to create an *egalitarian* property-owning democracy (Gamble and Kelly, 1996; White, 2003). Indeed, Pierson (1994) argues that Thatcher wanted the opposite, and used the sale of council housing to retrench the welfare state. He argues that Thatcher successfully used the 'right-to-buy' sale of council houses to sell off large parts of the public housing stock without replacement (see also Jones and Murie, 2006). Disney and Luo (2017) record that the right-to-buy sale of council properties was mainly responsible for a rise in the share of home-ownership among householders in the UK from 55 per cent in 1979 to 70 per cent in the early 2000s: 'Nonetheless, the spread of asset ownership due to right-to-buy is very uneven, with unskilled workers and low-income council tenants under-represented among right-to-buy purchasers' (Cole et al, 2015). Gamble and Kelly (1996: 81) write that 'The New Right idea of a property-owning democracy is a sham. Despite the attachment of the British Conservatives to the idea since the 1920s … the inequality of individual ownership and wealth holding persists.' Conservative versions of property-owning democracy stress individual responsibility but do not attend to the background inequalities that constrain individual choices.

A challenge remains of how an egalitarian property-owning democracy might be created. Piketty (2014) argues in *Capital in the 21st Century* that capital is the main source of inequality in the 21st century. Housing scholars argue that although there is greater recognition now that housing contributes to wealth inequality, policymakers have yet to develop adequate responses to these issues (Maclennan and Miao, 2017; Fernandez and Aalbers, 2017; Elsinga, 2017). Maclennan and Miao (2017: 128) comment that 'Housing policy-makers show little sign of engaging with the insights derived [from Piketty's work] ... not least the implication that core housing policies may be reinforcing rather than reducing inequalities within and between generations.'

Creating an egalitarian property-owning democracy implies at least two areas for common research. The first is the greater taxation of housing wealth. Elsinga (2017: 149) underlines the importance of taxing housing: 'New principles in policies for housing could start by tax policies taking housing equity into account aiming at acceptable social inequality.' Elsinga also argues that there is a need to outline new types of housing taxation. Housing will often form an important part of a person's final estate or inheritance, and so estate or inheritance taxes will involve the taxation of housing wealth (Ackerman and Alstott, 1999; Le Grand and Nissan, 2000; White, 2003; Atkinson, 2015). There is a long literature on models of property taxation (for an overview, see Mirrlees et al, 2011a). However, questions remain about which specific taxes ought to command priority, as well as how to turn tax ideas into reality.

Second, in developing new models of home-ownership, Conservative arguments dominate the ideology of owner-occupation and property-ownership (Gregory, 2016). Home-ownership is seen as important because it supports personal responsibility and self-reliance. The investor-subject approach fits this ideology of personal responsibility. Gregory (2016: 18) claims that shared ownership could be used to challenge an ideology based on individualism and self-reliance:

> The aim here would not simply be to offer a thin slice of the POD [property-owning democracy] to more people, but to shape a policy narrative around shared ownership in such a way that a positive story is told about its hybrid nature, bridging the often binary distinction between 'independent' owners and 'dependent' social tenants.

Developing different models of home-ownership can potentially reshape the ideology of home-ownership. Fox O'Mahony and

Overton (2015), for example, conducted qualitative research on the impact of equity release schemes among homeowners, and found that such schemes can often change the meaning of the home and home-ownership. Shared ownership models might therefore be used to challenge an investor-subject ideology.

Honoré (1961) outlines a classic account of the nature of ownership. He argues that ownership of an object usually involves 11 types of rights. These rights cover the possession, use, management, transmission and control of the object. Other rights include those over the capital value, income, security from expropriation, freehold, judgemental liability and duties not to harm others. Each of these rights may be shaped in a variety of ways. Honoré's list can no doubt be extended to include other rights as well. What is important here is that the different rights just mentioned can be combined in different ways and that this therefore gives rise to different models of ownership. There is a range of hybrid or shared ownership forms between pure private and common ownership (Whitehead, 2010; Whitehead and Monk, 2011).

Debates about housing equity stakes are one attempt to forge new agendas on ownership (Edwards, 2001; Whitehead et al, 2006). This could be used as a platform for further research between asset-based welfare and housing asset-based welfare. Housing equity stakes are admittedly a small part of total ownership forms. For example, Gregory (2016) notes that housing equity stakes only form 2 per cent of UK housing. One challenge, then, is to develop models that can be applied at a larger scale. Whitehead, Travers and Keilland (2006) highlight three types of housing equity stakes within asset-based welfare. The first is access models that try to help people to acquire and build up ownership, and encourage people to build up to full ownership rights. The second is savings schemes that try to use housing to build up personal savings. For example, tenants might be able to claim matched savings from public or private agencies for any money in addition to rent that they put in a special savings account. The third is cost reduction schemes that reduce the costs of living in a property (for example, rent reductions for those that live in a property for a certain length of time). Whitehead, Travers and Keilland (2006) argue that while access schemes typically benefit better-off tenants able to afford full ownership, savings or cost reduction schemes favour poorer tenants who are unable to afford full ownership.

If the aim is to develop new ownership forms, then further research ought to concentrate on savings or cost reduction schemes. The ultimate aim of access models is usually for people to gain full ownership rights, and so these approaches are not directed at developing hybrid ownership forms. Savings schemes combine rights over home-ownership with efforts to help tenants build a financial buffer, and so this blends together themes from housing asset-based welfare and asset-based welfare. Cost reduction schemes also have the potential for fashioning new ownership forms by allowing for different mixes of property rights.

Shared ownership could be used to challenge the growth of private landlordism. Private landlordism is likely to add to growing inequality as it allows private landlords to amass more wealth and income, and widens the gap between landlords and tenants. Maclennan and Miao (2017) state that addressing the housing gap between owners and non-owners is more important for reducing wealth inequality than focusing on the top 1 per cent of the wealth distribution. One way of reducing the impact of private landlordism on inequality is to fashion a model of shared ownership that curtails some of the rights associated with private property. Using Honoré's terms, a shared ownership form might mean qualifying rights over income and capital value from a property.

An alternative model of housing would seem to carry implications most obviously for capital markets. This would mean less emphasis upon borrowing to invest. Although home-ownership might still be deemed to be important, there is unlikely to be a relentless drive to create a nation of homeowners. This means that the volume and size of mortgage and private debt is likely to fall. There will also be a need for other financial products that would allow people to build equity stakes within housing. Financial services might then evolve to support collective forms of ownership.

An example: millennial angst

The preceding discussion suggests that developing a new model of housing may help break the grip of an investor-subject approach on public policy. Changes in housing are important as this is likely to impact upon the financial system. For example, an approach that stresses the significance of borrowing for investment is likely to fuel private debt. An alternative vision of housing may yield changes in the nature of borrowing markets.

This section applies some of these ideas to a real-world example. In particular, it looks at the problems that young people – millennials – face in buying a home in the UK. The challenges facing young people have sparked much comment and policy interest (Willetts, 2010; Intergenerational Commission, 2018). Although household wealth has grown very quickly during the 21st century, no generation born after 1960 in the UK is building more wealth than their predecessors. Earnings growth has stalled, with millennials – those born between 1981 and 2000 – earning the same as those born 15 years before them at the same age. Membership of defined benefit pension schemes at age 25 has halved for those born in the 1980s compared to those born in 1970. Millennials are also half as likely to own their own home at age 30 as those born between 1946 and 1965 (Intergenerational Commission, 2018). The difficulties that millennials face in buying a home feed into the growth of the private rental sector. Ronald et al (2017: 174) comment that the 'resurgence of private renting [is] driven by growing demand among younger adults excluded from home ownership, and the buying up of housing to let by those already in the market'.

The aim of public policy is not necessarily to encourage young people to be able to buy a home outright. The needs of millennials – and people more generally – might be met through a mix of full home-ownership and renting. Addressing this point means reflecting upon the significance of housing for most people. Arguably, the most basic role of housing is to provide people with shelter. As will be seen in Chapter 5, housing can be viewed as a consumption good whereby inhabitants consume the shelter and warmth of their home. Both rented accommodation and full ownership rights might provide people with adequate shelter. However, some form of ownership rights might guarantee inhabitants greater security over tenure. On Honoré's (1961) terms, this might correspond to rights over use. Allowing young people rights of use need not imply full rights over ownership. This might be achieved through a partial or shared ownership scheme. Any reform of housing in the UK has to face a situation where there is inequality in the ownership of housing wealth between the generations. This inequality can form a barrier to developing alternative models of housing.

The Resolution Foundation policy institute convened the Intergenerational Commission (2018) to make recommendations as regards tackling the gap between the young and the old. The former Conservative politician David Willetts chaired the Intergenerational Commission. His involvement reflected a long-standing interest in this area. Willetts (2010) wrote a book called *The Pinch* in which he claimed that a baby-boomer generation born between 1946 and 1965 had effectively pinched the rightful inheritance of their children. Changes in the global economy, technology and government policy might all have played a role in the fate of millennials. However, Willetts claims that older people are also to blame. The metaphor of the pinch places older people in the guise of thieves of their children's future. Willetts (2010: xv–xvi) states that:

> The charge is that the boomers have been guilty of a monumental failure to protect the interests of future generations. The baby boomers have concentrated wealth in the hands of their own generation. It is far harder for the younger generation to get started on the housing ladder or save for the future in a decent company pension.

The difficulties that millennials face in buying a home is arguably the main preoccupation of the Intergenerational Commission (2018). The report makes recommendations regarding pay, housing, pensions and the state. However, there are twice as many proposals in the section on housing than in each of the other areas.

The Intergenerational Commission (2018) cites the 18th-century thinker Edmund Burke as one of the inspirations for the idea of intergenerational fairness. In *Reflections on the Revolution in France*, Burke (1999 [1790]: 96) introduces the idea of society as a contract between different generations:

> Society is indeed a contract. ... It is partnership in all science; a partnership in all art; a partnership in every virtue, and in all perfection. As the ends of such a partnership cannot be obtained in many generations, it becomes a partnership not only between those who are living, but between those who are living, those who are dead, and those who are to be born.

Burke argues that there is a web of obligations and duties that has evolved between the generations. Families provide a concrete way of binding together different generations with the ties that exist between grandparents, parents and children. Families reproduce themselves over time and so are a way that society can itself be reproduced.

Burke highlights the importance of the transfer of property for the creation of a stable family identity. He writes that:

> The power of perpetuating our property in our families is one of the most valuable and interesting circumstances belonging to it, and that which tends the most to the perpetuation of society itself. It makes our weakness subservient to our virtue; it grafts benevolence even upon avarice. The possessors of family wealth, and of

the distinction which attends hereditary possession (as most concerned in it) are the natural securities for this transmission. (Burke, 1999 [1790]: 51)

Here, Burke makes a direct link between inheritance and the perpetuation of society. He suggests that inheritance promotes individual virtue, for example, when parents care about the welfare of their children. Burke supports the transfer of property across the generations. For Burke, this signals the perpetuation of family and also of society. Property can take many forms but the most relevant type here is home-ownership.

Two things may be important for addressing the housing gap among the young. The first is a redistribution of housing wealth from baby-boomers to millennials. This redistribution is likely to involve the taxation of wealth. Chapter 5 considers the practicality of taxing wealth such as housing. The second is opening up new debates about the nature of home-ownership. Burke refers to the web of ties and the unwritten understandings between the generations. One such area for exploration concerns the meaning of home-ownership. Ownership is a complex bundle of rights and duties, and it is possible to devise many different types of ownership. Neoliberals are interested in housing as a type of investment good. Indeed, the language that neoliberals use to refer to housing may be revealing as they tend to describe this as an asset or property rather than a family home.

Burke might provide a spur for alternative views of home-ownership. The 'family home' is a trope of conservative thought. Former Chancellor George Osborne invoked this idea when he presented Conservative Party plans to raise the threshold for paying inheritance tax to £1 million as taking the family home out of this tax. The concept of the family home might be used to open up debates about the nature of home-ownership. The family home points to a particular type of collective ownership, where the family is the collective unit. Unpacking what might be meant by the family could be used to explore the different rights and duties associated with collective ownership, and it may be possible to devise hybrid forms of ownership. This exploration of alternative ownership forms may be useful for fixing millennial bugs.

Conclusion

Borrowing to invest is a key part of an investor-subject approach. Arguably, the most important manifestation of this approach is in housing. Governments in places such as the UK and US emphasised expanding home-ownership among the population. Improved access to mortgage markets was one of the things that made this a reality. Critics argue that this stress on home-ownership fuelled a rise in personal indebtedness. This trend points to the ways that different policy areas – in this case, housing – have an impact on involvement in the financial system.

The risk that financial inclusion may be tied to this approach to home-ownership should not be ignored. This chapter has suggested that this is not the only relationship that might exist between housing and credit markets. It suggests that different models of home-ownership might be used to underpin a different relationship between the housing and financial systems.

5

Alternatives

Introduction

This chapter looks at financial inclusion and alternative agendas. Chapter 4 suggested that different models of home-ownership might be used to challenge the grip of investor-subjects within housing and the financial system. The present chapter extends this discussion of alternatives. Chapter 1 claimed that it is possible to disentangle financialisation from neoliberalism. The suggestion, then, is that it is possible to develop different versions of financial inclusion (and financialisation) that do not lead necessarily to neoliberalism.

One understanding of different agendas might conceive of this as alternatives *to* financial inclusion. This book has noted that supporters of financial inclusion claim that it reduces the poverty premium from being denied access to mainstream financial services. The poverty premium shows a concern with poverty and inequality. However, there may be different ways of reducing poverty and inequality. Critics of financial inclusion may claim that there are better ways of supporting equality than financial inclusion.

One task, then, might be to compare financial inclusion with other policy agendas. A prelude to comparative research of this kind is to set out the different policy agendas on offer. This chapter sets out two of the most obvious possible alternatives to those considered in this book. First, this chapter outlines the role of a universal basic income. Chapter 2 suggests that a nexus exists between money, financial capability and access to the financial system. Lack of money might render the capacity to make financial decisions and access to the financial system fairly meaningless. Some observers may prefer simply to concentrate on increasing money to individuals and households rather than paying attention to enhancing financial capability or access to financial services. A universal basic income is one way of ensuring that all citizens have access to money. Second, the chapter outlines universal basic services. Critics of a great risk shift from the state to individuals often prefer to consolidate and extend the welfare state. Universal basic services have been proposed as one significant way of extending the welfare state.

The discussion of these alternatives could be a basis for future comparative research. This chapter suggests that financial inclusion can play an important role in supporting these alternatives. This chapter first sketches out the main parts of a universal basic income. A universal basic income is a related policy to the CTF discussed in Chapter 3. Indeed, one set of debates compares a basic income to basic capital. This highlights the overlaps between a universal basic income and some of the financial inclusion policies considered in this book. The chapter then suggests that access to the financial system is likely to be important for making a basic income a reality.

Universal basic services are a more comprehensive alternative to a universal basic income as the latter is a single policy. However, the term 'universal basic services' alludes to universal basic income and so points to links between these proposals. The chapter argues that the financial system is likely to be an important part of universal basic services and also discusses how universal basic services and universal basic income might be combined.

One challenge facing any reformist programme is whether reforms are feasible as well as desirable. The remainder of the chapter considers issues of feasibility by examining the greater taxation of housing wealth. Examining this case is interesting as Chapter 4 suggested that the greater taxation of property is one way of creating a more egalitarian property-owning democracy. Taxing wealth more heavily might also be important for the alternative policies considered in this chapter.

Universal basic income

Published during the 15th century, Thomas More's (2020 [1516]) *Utopia* is often cited as a forerunner for a basic income. More described an imaginary society without private property but where people's needs, such as food, are met by the community (Piachaud, 2018). A universal basic income promises 'regular, non-means-tested cash transfers to all residents of a political territory on an individual basis, without means-test or work requirement' (Haagh, 2019: 243). A universal basic income has five key parts: it is regular; it is paid in cash; it is provided to the individual; it is universal, with no means test; and it is unconditional, having no requirement to work or seek work (Piachaud, 2018; Haagh, 2019). For example, Standing (2019) proposes that one version of a universal basic income might involve paying all adults in the UK £100 per week and all children £50 a week.

A wide range of arguments have been advanced in favour of a universal basic income. One set of arguments is rooted in liberal thought and insist that a universal basic income is needed to provide real freedom for all. This means that people need a regular income to be genuinely free to pursue whatever life they choose (Van Parijs, 1991, 1997; Van Parijs and Vanderborght, 2017). Other strands build on sociology or the changing nature of the economy. One strand links the case for a universal basic income to the impact of automation or robots on the economy. Automation is thought to threaten all types of jobs in the economy, from the use of robots for performing routine tasks on factory production lines to the use of computer algorithms to provide professional services such as legal advice. Although automation might displace jobs, proponents argue that it may also create surplus within the economy. The idea is to then spread this surplus throughout society through a universal basic income (Susskind, 2020a, 2020b).

A full basic income has yet to be implemented anywhere in the world (De Wispelaere, 2016a, 2016b; Piachaud, 2018). Piachaud (2018: 309) records that 'The idea of a Basic Income is not new but no nation has introduced a universal, unconditional Basic Income.' There have been trials or pilots of parts of a basic income scheme in places such as Finland, Uganda and Brazil but most of the empirical analyses rely on simulations rather than studies of an actual policy (De Wispelaere, 2016a, 2016b; Martinelli, 2017a, 2017b; Downes and Lansley, 2018; Halmetoja et al, 2018).

Basic income and basic capital

A universal basic income promises to provide citizens with regular money payments. A basic income is a flow of income and this differs from the sort of asset-based welfare policies discussed in Chapter 3. Nevertheless, a universal basic income has a family resemblance to policies such as capital grants (Ackerman and Alstott, 1999; Ackerman et al, 2005). Signs of this can be seen in one of the chief writers of the modern literature on capital grants. In particular, during the 18th century, Thomas Paine (1987 [1797]) outlined a theory of justice in his pamphlet 'Agrarian justice'. Paine argued that justice meant that a person should receive a £15 grant when they are 21 and £10 each year once they are 50. The wealth of each generation would be taxed to provide payments for the next generation, thereby making a link between the taxation of wealth and the provision of assets and income to all.

Arguably, Paine (1987 [1797]) anticipated modern interest in the merits of basic income versus basic capital for achieving equality for all (Cunliffe and Errygers, 2003; Ackerman and Alstott, 2004; Ackerman et al, 2005; White, 2011, 2015; Olin Wright, 2004, 2015). Ackerman and Alstott (1999) propose that all US citizens should receive an US$80,000 grant once they are 21 years old. Atkinson (2015) outlines a recent version of these liberal–egalitarian ideas in his call to revive the CTF to reduce wealth inequality. For Atkinson (2015), basic capital is one of 15 proposals aimed at fulfilling Paine's dream of an inheritance for all. He proposes the introduction of a lifetime capital receipts tax (which taxes the gifts or inheritances that a person receives over their life) as a way of paying for grants for all, with revenue from current inheritance tax receipts in the UK providing for a grant of around £5,000 for all. White (2015) claims that basic capital is preferable to basic income as it has greater potential to transform a person's life. Olin Wright (2015) counters that basic income is superior to basic capital because it has greater potential to transform the capitalist system.

The financial system and basic income or basic capital

Access to a bank or savings account is likely to be a precondition for any well-functioning basic income or basic capital scheme. For example, governments must have some way of providing citizens with regular income payments in a basic income scheme. These payments are likely to occur in a bank account. Similarly, a basic capital payment will probably be deposited into some form of savings account. Thus, financial inclusion can be considered part of the supporting framework for either a basic income or basic capital scheme. Put another way, financial inclusion provides a pipeline through which money payments can be made.

Financial inclusion might also be important more broadly for expanding the choices available to citizens under either a basic income or basic capital scheme. Access to the financial system can allow people to convert one type of policy into the other. People might be able to use their regular stream of income payments to borrow a single larger lump sum. Conversely, people might be able to use a lump sum to buy an annuity that provides a guaranteed stream of income payments. To give an idea of the sort of income stream one might expect from a capital grant, the UK government's free and impartial advice service, Pension Wise, estimates that a person with a £100,000 pension pot and retiring at age 66 years old in 2018 could expect to receive an annual taxable income of £4,200 (see: www.pensionwise.gov.uk/en/guaranteed-income). With appropriate access to financial goods and services, basic income and basic capital could belong to the same continuum of policies (Fitzpatrick, 2011; White, 2011). Indeed, White

(2011) proposes a hybrid policy that combines parts of basic capital and basic income.

Financial capability might also be important for basic income or basic capital. This might be seen by debates over 'stakeblowing'. One concern voiced about basic capital is that citizens might 'blow' their stake in one go through decisions that they later come to regret. For example, a young person might 'blow' an US$80,000 grant on wild parties. Sometimes, this is presented as a case for a basic income. A regular set of income payments offers citizens an insurance against decisions they later come to regret as they can always make different choices with future payments. Ackerman and Alstott (1999) respond to this point by proposing that citizens should not receive their US$80,000 grant until they have graduated with a high-school diploma. This links receipt of a grant with a minimum level of educational attainment. This makes a link to individual capacity to make financial choices and shows how financial capability might also be considered part of the practical support for their stakeholder grant idea.

Universal basic services

A recent twist in debates are calls for universal basic services over a universal basic income. Universal basic services refer to collectively funded public services that are free at the point of use (Percy, 2017; Coote et al, 2019; Gough, 2019). Here, the starting point is the idea that 'A modern economy needs a social safety net that is just as modern, and one that is more flexible and effective than the conditional benefits system we have inherited' (Percy, 2017: 9). The core idea of universal basic services is that seven core public services are provided free at the point of delivery. These are healthcare, education, legal and democracy, shelter, food, transport, and information. Some of the services are familiar as they are already universal and provided free at the point of delivery in a number of countries. For example, the UK National Health Service (NHS) provides healthcare services free at the point of delivery and available to all. Similarly, the state education system through primary and secondary schools is also universal and free to use. The legal and democracy service refers to a common legal and democratic framework throughout society.

Of course, the picture is more complex when looking at the detail in each of these areas. For example, in the UK, there are certain limited areas within healthcare that are not free at the point of delivery. Certain groups of patients face limited prescription charges for their medications.

Similarly, with education, students may have to pay tuition fees at university. Future debate over universal basic services may examine which exact services are provided free at the point of delivery for all.

Although it is important to acknowledge these complexities, the main thrust of the universal basic services approach is to provide the aforementioned services free at the point of use for all. This means that the model of universal basic services builds on and extends an already-existing set of such services. For transport, one aim here is to provide a 'freedom pass' for all that would guarantee free access for all to bus services. On food, the aim would be to provide one third of the meals (breakfast, lunch or dinner) for those households that struggle with feeding themselves each day. For shelter, the proposal is to expand the stock of social housing and this new housing would be based on need and offered at zero rent, have an allowance for utilities, and be exempt from property taxes such as Council Tax (CT) in the UK. Finally, information would provide free basic phone and Internet access to all citizens.

This also has similarities with a 'foundational economy' approach (Bentham et al, 2013; Foundation Economy Collective, 2018). The foundational economy is the joint work of a team of scholars interested in exploring alternatives to neoliberalism. The foundational economy refers to the basic infrastructure that forms the foundation of most economies. This infrastructure covers utilities such as water, gas and telecommunications networks. The idea of this infrastructure also covers important parts of the financial system, such as banking. This approach claims that the well-being of citizens 'depends less on individual consumption and more on their social consumption of essential goods and services – from water and retail banking, to schools and care homes – in what we call *the foundational economy*' (Foundation Economy Collective, 2018: 1, emphasis in original). The preceding definition accepts that banking is part of the foundational economy and stresses its social or collective character. An original manifesto for the foundational economy declares that banking is 'just as much an utility as electricity in a society of card payments and mass credit' (Bentham et al, 2013: 9).

A needs-based rationale for universal basic services

Gough (2019) argues that it is important to develop a sound theoretical and moral framework for universal basic services; otherwise, it will be vulnerable to being chipped away at by its critics. He outlines one such argument that draws on his work on the theory of human needs.

His argument progresses in three main stages. First, he says that it is important to fashion a model of individual agency. He argues that economists prioritise the significance of individual wants in their approach to agency: 'Economic theory gives … preference to the wants individuals happen to have, whether these are assumed to derive from an individual's innate preferences or their cultural and economic environment' (Gough, 2019: 535). For orthodox economic theory, the task is to then add up or aggregate individual preferences. He argues for a different model of human agency. Gough (2019) argues that it is important to examine what resources do for individuals rather than simply relying on individual wants. Gough (2019) argues that both Amartya Sen's capability theory and 'need theory' should be the basis of universal basic services. He writes that to 'gain a strong purchase on UBS [universal basic services], we must turn to two other schools of thought – capability theory and need theory' (Gough, 2019: 2). Sen's capability theory was discussed in Chapter 2. Gough's (2019) need theory proposes that people have a basic set of needs that are essential for any participation in social life. Examples of these universal basic needs include nutrition, shelter, health, social participation (covering education and information), physical security and income security.

Second, Gough (2019) highlights the importance of contemporary need satisfiers or systems of provision. He says that these are the systems or networks that help realise universal needs. For example, he cites food security and diets as satisfiers for nutrition. He claims that the attention to need satisfiers invokes a view of the economy as a set of networks or systems.

Third, he proposes a number of principles to guide public provision. He argues that these should be based on ideas of equality, efficiency, sustainability and solidarity. Although Gough (2019) accepts that there may be a range of institutions that satisfy these principles, he prefers collective forms of provision.

Gough's (2019) argument implies a role for the financial system. He cites income security as a universal human need and acknowledges that the financial system is important for providing income security. Gough (2019) claims that contemporary need satisfiers for income security include income maintenance and money and payment systems. For example, governments may need to make benefit payments to maintain income. Gough (2019) refers to private insurance, retail banking and social security as provisioning systems. Therefore, he accepts that parts of the financial system may play a role within universal basic services. This does not mean that he necessarily endorses present policies or institutions. For example, a publicly owned banking system might be deemed preferable to a plethora of competing private banks. Similarly, it might be possible to develop different models of insurance. Nevertheless, the financial system is important for sustaining income security. One might also extend his approach by noting that savings and responsible lending might also be important for maintaining income security by ensuring that people have a financial cushion to fall back on or can borrow at reasonable rates if they face a sudden drop in income.

Combining universal basic services and universal basic income

Gough (2019) outlines an important case for universal basic services. He is critical of a universal basic income, though, as he claims that it distracts reformists from more urgent priorities. He says that:

> The underlying belief or dream is that basic income will provide a mobilising theme to bring about radical change. ... Similar proposals have been made every few years for the last 50 years and they have got nowhere. The problem is that it combines a radical vision with a naive or insouciant view of politics. ... I fear that this latest plan will drain the energies of the left in social policy and will divert attention from so many other worthwhile policy alternatives: the living wage, boosting trade unionism, free childcare, radical changes in housing policy, policies to reduce working time to limit turbo-consumption, green investment and so on. (Gough 2016)

Gough (2016) is right that trade-offs will be inevitable when there are many competing policies but only limited public resources. His preference is to explore a wide variety of alternatives instead of a basic income. A different possibility, though, is to combine a universal basic income with other policies. This stance does not deny that trade-offs are important. Reformists may still have to make choices over a basic income versus other policies. However, there may be reasons for seeing basic income as part of wider package of reforms (Haagh, 2011; Percy, 2017).

Haagh (2011) argues that both social democracy and basic income try to enhance the control that a person has over time. She says that control over time recognises the importance of the choices that people make over employment, leisure and care over the life cycle. Haagh (2011) presents a person's control over time as an important part of individual freedom. She suggests that a basic income gives people some control over time within markets. However, she argues that social democracy also enhances a person's control over time by removing them from market pressures. Her view of social democracy invokes a strong welfare state, which is implied by universal basic services. She claims that:

> Both social democracy and the basic income reform entail commitments to advance individuals' control of time through decommodification. The basic income does this more fully in respect to the rights to (a basic) independent income, but social democracy adds to this through ways that participation in production is made less market dependent and unreliable than the case in liberal states. Therefore, seeing the basic income as in conjunction with social democracy is preferable to seeing basic income as a standalone institution. (Haagh, 2011: 49)

Similarly, Percy (2017) presents universal basic services and universal basic income as complementary policies.

It is important to acknowledge the tensions or problems that might exist when trying to combine a universal basic income with universal basic services. Collectivist ideas are a defining theme of universal basic services and, more widely, the welfare state (Bergmann, 2004, 2008; Haagh, 2011; Portes, 2017). Haagh (2011) records that the welfare state embodies an idea of social insurance that guarantees collective support for each citizen if faced by a specific hardship, such as unemployment. Solidarity between citizens underpins the role of social insurance in protecting each citizen. Haagh (2011: 45) writes that 'Social insurance and its twin idea, solidarity, represent more encompassing egalitarian principles than equal shares, of which the basic income – like citizens' pensions or child grants – is a typical case.'

Basic income is much more individualist in nature than universal basic services. This does not mean that collectivist ideas are entirely absent in a universal basic income, for example, as it involves the collective funding of income to each citizen. Nevertheless, individualism is much more prominent within a universal basic income than universal basic services. One sign of this is the way that the basic income idea has won support from advocates of free markets in ways that universal basic services do not (Friedman, 1962; Lehto, 2018). For example, Milton Friedman's (1962) negative income tax proposal is a version of a basic income that resonates with some neoliberals. Similarly, a pamphlet published by the London-based free market think-tank the Adam Smith Institute backs a universal basic income (Lehto, 2018).

Another issue is over the timing or sequence of any package of reforms. The Social Prosperity Network's (2017) model of universal basic services involves seven public services. However, this model might be extended in various ways. For example, their approach does not call for universal and free childcare. Bergmann (2004, 2008) claims that the provision of free childcare highlights the varying impacts of a basic income and the welfare state on gender inequality. She says that whereas a universal basic income expands the opportunities for leisure, free childcare increases the options for paid employment. She claims that the opportunities for paid employment promise to be more beneficial for women than a basic income. Bergmann (2004: 117) argues that concerns about gender equality provide a case for extending the welfare state before any basic income reforms: 'The fully developed welfare state deserves priority over Basic Income because it accomplishes what Basic Income does not: it guarantees that certain specific human needs will be met. ... When this has been accomplished, then will be the time to consider starting to phase in Basic Income.' Of course, one might also invoke other trade-offs when considering the timing of reforms. For example, the relative costs of a universal basic income and universal basic services may impact on the sequence of any reforms. Reed and Percy (2017) estimate that current spending on four universal basic services in the UK (health, education, transport and housing) represents 41 per cent of total government spending and total government spending is about 41 per cent of gross domestic product. Percy (2017) records that the extra spending that would be needed in the UK to provide the full set of universal basic services would amount to about £42.16 billion. Reed and Percy (2017) estimate that a tax-free basic income payment of £20 a week would yield an annual cost of £10 billion. De Henau (2017) says that providing free and universal childcare in the UK would cost between £33 billion and £55 billion. It might be easier politically to implement a cheaper basic income option than more costly universal basic services.

The practicality of alternatives: the case of taxing wealth

The preceding discussion suggests that financial inclusion can be used to sustain an egalitarian agenda. However, this claim also raises questions of the feasibility of shaping such an agenda. This section turns to this claim by looking at the case of taxing wealth. Chapter 4 discussed the prospect of taxing housing wealth as a way of developing a new agenda on housing. As such, the rest of this chapter looks particularly at an example of the taxation of property and it looks at the Welsh government's reform of CT in the mid-2000s.

The study of the Welsh government reform of CT also contributes to research on the financialisation of the state. The literature on financialisation suggests that there is a need for further work on the role that the state plays in extending or limiting financial markets. Van der Zwan (2014) argues that research on this will involve examining the strategies adopted by different interest groups in pressing for reform. Case-study research can contribute to this broad agenda. Studying how the Welsh government managed to increase the tax on housing may be part of this programme.

The 'tyranny of the status quo' is commonly seen as an important block on tax reform. The tyranny of the status quo refers to the idea that government tax reforms will usually provoke a strong reaction from those that 'lose' from the reform but little support from those that 'win' from the reform. This creates a bias whereby the government is reluctant to reform taxes and so sticks to the status quo (Muellbauer and Cameron, 2000; Lyons, 2007; Mirrlees et al, 2011a, 2011b; Johnson and Myles, 2011).

A striking example of this tyranny of the status quo is the general failure to reform CT in the UK. CT is the main tax on property in the UK. Properties are placed in one of eight CT bands depending on the price of the property relative to other properties. Band A is the lowest-value property band and band H is the highest-value property value band. CT bills are expressed as ratios of the band D CT bill. The ratios are expressed in ninths, which means as a fraction of nine. The bill for a band H property is 18/9 (or double) the band D bill. The bill for band A property is 6/9 the band D bill. This means that the CT bill for band H is triple the CT bill for band A. CT bills also reflect charges for local government services such as rubbish collection and so is a hybrid tax combining a tax on property with charges for local services (Jones et al, 2006a, 2006b; Lyons, 2007). There is a 25 per cent CT bill reduction for sole occupiers, and income support through Council Tax Benefit is made available for low-income groups (Adam and Browne, 2012).

A common idea is to revalue CT to reflect large changes in property prices since CT was first introduced (Kenway and Palmer, 1999; Plimmer, 1999; Muellbauer and Cameron, 2000; Jones et al, 2006a, 2006b; Lyons, 2007; Mirrlees et al, 2011a, 2011b; European Commission, 2014). The tyranny of the status quo seems to be a key block to reforming CT. Mirrlees et al (2011a: 383) note that 'any revaluation inevitably creates losers and winners – and losers tend to be very vocal. This is one of the most egregious demonstrations of the "tyranny of the status quo" as a block to desirable change.'

An important exception to the tyranny of the status quo is the Welsh government's revaluation of CT in 2005. Since devolution, UK government CT policy only applies to England and Wales. The Scottish Parliament has the remit for local government finance and Northern Ireland has its own system of domestic rates that differ from CT. Up to 2011, the Welsh government was dependent upon the UK government for enabling legislation for CT reform in Wales (National Assembly for Wales, 2011). Wales is the only part of the UK that has seen a revaluation of CT. This revaluation was introduced on 1 April 2005 and is based on property values on 1 April 2003. This revaluation updated the existing eight CT bands and added a new band I for very high-value properties.

How was the Welsh revaluation of CT possible and what lessons does it contain for tax reform more generally? This chapter claims that the tyranny of the status quo is not a fixed law. Government can play a role in shaping this constraint by framing how winners and losers from reform are understood. The Welsh government's 2005 revaluation showed that CT reform is possible. Its failure to communicate the complexity of reform hampered efforts to reform CT in 2015.

Background

The failure of the Community Charge, or 'Poll Tax', provides the immediate background to the introduction of CT in the early 1990s. During the 1980s, there was a system of domestic rates for UK households that were based on the value of property. Although the rates were well understood and fairly easy to collect, the Conservative government was critical of the rates because they did not take account of the number of people in a household. This meant that sole householders in an expensive property might pay larger rates than a many-person household in a cheaper property. Prime Minister Margaret Thatcher saw this as unfair and wanted to replace the rates with a tax on persons. The Poll Tax led to mass avoidance and public riots in London. The failure of the Poll Tax has been described as one of the largest policy blunders by a UK government since the end of the Second World War and was a key factor in the deposal of Thatcher as Conservative leader (Butler et al, 1994; King and Crewe, 2014).

CT was introduced as the replacement for the Poll Tax. The aim was not to return to the rates and so the CT was based on relative property prices. Repeated calls have been made for the reform of CT (Kenway and Palmer, 1999; Plimmer, 1999; Muellbauer and Cameron, 2000; Jones et al, 2006a, 2006b; Lyons, 2007; Mirrlees et al, 2011a, 2011b; European Commission, 2014). Sir James Mirrlees chaired a review of the principles that should shape the design of tax systems in the 21st century. This review argued that tax systems should be both progressive and neutral. Progressivity means that richer people should pay a higher proportion of their income or wealth than poorer people on taxation. This springs from a commitment to equality, as well as a belief that richer people have a greater capacity to pay higher taxes than poorer people. Neutrality means that similar economic activities should be taxed similarly. Neutrality is aimed at ensuring an efficient tax system.

Although Mirrlees et al (2011a, 2011b) outlined general tax reforms, the review illustrates their ideas by proposing reforms of UK taxation. Mirrlees et al (2011a, 2011b) argue that housing should ideally be taxed as a consumption good. This is because housing provides a range of services that people consume (such as shelter or warmth). Mirrlees et al (2011a) propose a Housing Services Tax (HST) to tax housing as a consumption good. They say that the HST should ideally be set at the same rate as general consumption tax in the UK (that is, Value Added Tax (VAT)). The HST would replace CT and other taxes on property in the UK. Mirrlees et al (2011a) propose that the HST would be a flat-rate percentage imposed on the rental value of the property (this would cover both rented and owner-occupied properties). Mirrlees et al (2011a) estimate that the HST would therefore be about 12 per cent of the value of housing services. They say that this rate was below the (then) level of VAT of 17.5 per cent but there may be scope for increasing the HST over time to approach the VAT rate.

Mirrlees et al (2011a, 2011b) acknowledge that reforming existing taxes is more likely than the implementation of HST. Mirrlees et al (2011a, 2011b) note that CT is highly regressive over property values and so violates their progressivity principle. In England, the threshold value for a band H property is £320,000 and the upper limit for a band A property is £40,000. Thus, the CT bill for a band H property is triple the value for a band A property but the value for a band H property is at least eight times the value of a band A property. CT is also based on property prices that are over 20 years out of date. There have been large relative house price changes and so current CT bands are out of date. Lyons (2007) notes that while revaluation might reduce regressivity over property values, this might not have much impact on regressivity over income (before income support through Council Tax Benefit is applied). This is because there are a class of 'asset-rich, income-poor' people who have lower incomes but live in higher-value properties. Lyons (2007) notes that these 'asset-rich, income-poor' people often include pensioners and form a minority of households. Lyons (2007) adds that the presence of such people does not undermine the case for revaluation, but highlights that the overall effect of revaluation on regressivity is ambiguous.

Mirrlees et al (2011a; 2011b) add that CT is inefficient. The 25 per cent discount on CT bills for sole occupiers provides incentives for the inefficient use of the existing housing stock by encouraging sole rather than multiple occupancy. Lack of regular revaluations might also contribute to instability in the housing market. Without regular revaluations, CT bills as a share of property values fall faster in areas in high property price growth than low property price growth. This would then mean that CT would not dampen property price booms (Muellbauer and Cameron, 2000; Jones et al, 2006a, 2006b). Jones et al (2006a, 2006b) simulate the likely effects of a CT revaluation on local government finances and the movement of properties between bands. They base their research on data from Scottish local authorities. Jones et al (2006a, 2006b) argue that CT revaluation could have a significant impact on local government finances and the movement of properties between bands. This is because CT bands focus on relative property values rather than being based on the capital value of a house. Jones et al (2006a, 2006b) conclude that CT revaluation would be more than 'rearranging the deckchairs'.

The tyranny of the status quo

The tyranny of the status quo claims that politicians can expect little thanks from the winners from tax reform but a strong backlash from those who lose out. However, winners and losers can be understood in different ways. Winners might be seen as those people that make a financial gain from a tax change. The financial gain might be understood to be the gain that arises from a specific tax change or from the wider impact that a particular tax change triggers for the whole tax system (for example, a tax rise might allow other taxes to be streamlined or cut) (Kaplow, 2011). Alternatively, winning might be associated with the way that tax reforms advance certain values. For example, a person might back a rise in the rate of income tax even though they are made financially worse off because this leads to a more progressive tax system that they support. This discussion is important because it means that governments may have a role in shaping how winners and losers from tax reform are understood in public debates.

The complexity of picking winners and losers may be seen by considering CT revaluation. If revaluation occurs, then an obvious set of winners and losers may be those properties that, respectively, drop down or rise up the CT bands. However, winners might also include properties that stay in the same band. The band that a particular property is placed in after revaluation depends on any changes in the property price relative to other property price changes. A property may stay in the same CT band if its property price rise is less than the rises elsewhere. If the revaluation is not aimed at raising more revenue overall, then the CT bill for a property that remains in the same band depends on the number of other properties that have changed bands. For example, a case where 50 per cent of properties stay in the same band but 25 per cent of properties drop down a band and 25 per cent of properties rise up a band may mean that the CT bill will be unchanged for a property that stays in the same band. The CT bill for a property that stays in the same band may rise if 5 per cent of properties rise up a band, 50 per cent of properties stay in the same band and 45 per cent of properties drop down a band.

A failure to revalue also creates winners and losers. This is because CT bills for properties that experience above-average rises in value are lower than they would be after revaluation. Properties with little or no rise in property values are, in effect, subsidising the CT bills of properties with high rises (Lyons, 2007; Mirrlees et al, 2011a, 2011b).

The 2005 CT revaluation in Wales

The Labour government passed the Local Government Act 2003, which promised a CT revaluation in England in 2007 and Wales in 2005. Thereafter, there would be a regular cycle of CT revaluations no longer than ten years after the previous revaluation. Although the Local Government Act 2003 provided a timetable for regular CT revaluations, successive UK ministers postponed a CT revaluation in England. CT revaluations were due in Wales in 2005 and 2015.

In 2000, the Welsh government published 'Simplifying the system: local government finance in Wales' (National Assembly for Wales, 2000), which outlined various options for local finance in Wales. One of the options mentioned was a revaluation of CT bands. The aim of such a reform was not to raise more money, but to make CT more progressive. The Welsh government followed up 'Simplifying the system: local government finance in Wales' with a policy paper in 2002 called *Freedom and Responsibility in Local Government* (Welsh Government, 2002a). This policy paper was developed in discussion with the Welsh Local Government Association (WLGA). *Freedom and Responsibility in Local Government* echoed the importance of having a more progressive CT.

The Welsh government then set up a Council Tax Revaluation Working Group (CTRWG) to advise on the policy options. The CTRWG had members nominated by the Welsh government, WLGA and Valuation Office Agency. The CTRWG held five meetings between May 2002 and October 2002. The work of the CTRWG was to feed into a consultation paper to be published by the Welsh government on CT reform (Consultative Forum on Finance, 2002).

The remit of the CTRWG states that the aim of reform was not to raise more money for local government, but to have a more progressive CT (CTRWG, 2002a). The CTRWG was asked to consider a transitional relief scheme that would help those properties that moved up bands following the revaluation. This attention to transitional relief highlights the concern the Welsh government had for helping those properties that faced the prospect of higher bills, as well as showing special concern with those properties that moved between bands. This also associates losers with properties that move between bands. The CTRWG considered three main policy choices. The first was to reallocate properties based on current values within existing bands. Modelling requested by the CTRWG showed that this would mean 51 per cent of properties would move up at least one band while 38 per cent would stay in the same band. The second policy choice was to revalue CT bands. Initial research suggested that this would mean little change to the overall tax base and 21 per cent of properties moving up at least one band. The third policy choice was to revalue bands and add new bands. This considered a new band A– at the bottom of the scale and a band H+ at the top of the scale. The CTRWG also considered the effects of varying the proportions attached to CT bands from ninths to eighths, tenths or 15ths (CTRWG, 2002a, 2002b, 2002c). Early predictions suggested that about a fifth of properties would move up bands by revaluing CT.

On 19 December 2002, the Welsh government published a first consultation on its plans to reform CT. This consultation outlined two main ideas for discussion: first, to revalue the existing bands and add a new band I at the top of the scale; and, second, to consider moving from a system of ninths to eighths to support progressive reform (Welsh Government, 2002b). The Welsh government notes that 66 per cent of responses backed a new band I and 45 per cent preferred to stay with a system of ninths (with 23 per cent preferring a move to eighths and 31 per cent not expressing a preference) (Welsh Government, 2004a, 2004b).

A second consultation document was published in June 2003. This supplementary consultation said that the Welsh government had decided not to move to a system of eighths as this would have meant many taxpayers having to pay more money. Although a move to eighths would improve the progressive nature of CT, the Welsh government anticipated that this move would mean higher CT bills for many people and so create many losers from reform. The Welsh government was concerned with avoiding this and so ruled out a move to eighths. A revalued set of CT bands was set out in the first consultation. There would be a new band I. The bands were set at 50 per cent of the difference between the average sale values. However, as the Welsh government revised the values for the CT bands, it wanted to have a supplementary consultation on the revised CT bands (Welsh Government, 2003).

The proposals set out in the second consultation document were broadly supported by county councils and the WLGA, though there were also calls for relief to be provided to help people and councils cope with a change to a new system. One of the Welsh government's key partners was therefore also concerned with the potential losers from reform and wanted policies in place to cushion rises in CT bills (Welsh Government, 2004a).

The VOA was responsible for revaluing properties as part of the reform. This involved revaluing about 1.3 million properties and placing these in the new bands. Initial work on placing properties in the bands began in April 2003 and the process ended in June 2004. The VOA drew up lists based on property values on 1 April 2003 (Valuation Office Agency, 2005). Official data show that prior to revaluation, CT revenue raised £924.1 million in 2004/05, and after revaluation, it raised £1,012 million. A Welsh government note to the Office of the Deputy Prime Minister noted that the average tax base rose by 5.4 per cent following the revaluation. About 1 per cent of this was attributed to the normal growth of the tax base and 4.4 per cent to the effects of the revaluation (Welsh Government, 2005a).

Effects of the 2005 revaluation

Tables 5.1 and 5.2 show the effects of the 2005 revaluation on the numbers of properties in the different bands. Table 5.1 reports the CT bands before and after the revaluation, and Table 5.2 shows the

Table 5.1: Council Tax bands in Wales

Council Tax band	Property values (£), Wales (1993)	Property values (£), Wales (2005)
A	Under 30,000	Under 44,000
B	30,001 to 39,000	44,001 to 65,000
C	39,001 to 51,000	65,001 to 91,000
D	50,001 to 66,000	91,001 to 123,000
E	66,001 to 90,000	123,001 to 162,000
F	90,001 to 120,000	162,001 to 223,000
G	120,001 to 240,000	223,001 to 324,000
H	240,001 and above	324,001 to 424,001
I	N/A	424,001 and above

Table 5.2: Number of properties in different Council Tax bands in Wales

Council Tax band	1993 list	2005 list
A	255,840	199,480
B	325,900	284,490
C	265,000	289,030
D	200,520	206,120
E	164,120	168,260
F	64,450	103,280
G	38,250	49,190
H	3,390	12,050
I	N/A	5,550

numbers of properties in Wales in the different CT bands before and after the revaluation. The second column of Table 5.2 shows the number of properties in each band after the inflows and outflows of properties following revaluation. The inflows (and outflows) are made up of properties that have either risen or fallen from other bands. The mix of inflows and outflows differs for different bands.

The Welsh government estimated that the majority of properties would either stay in the same band or drop bands following revaluation (Welsh Government, 2005b). It estimated that 50 per cent of properties would stay in the same band, 25 per cent of properties would drop down the bands and 25 per cent of properties would rise up the bands. Following the revaluation, more properties than expected rose up bands and fewer properties than expected dropped down bands. Less than a quarter of the expected number of properties dropped down the bands and there were four times as many properties that rose bands as those properties that fell down bands. A total of 773,310 out of 1,317,450 properties stayed in the same band following the revaluation. This means that about 59 per cent of all properties stayed in the same band. A total of 438,760 properties moved up at least one band following the revaluation, which is about 33 per cent of all properties (Valuation Office Agency, 2015). Around 8 per cent of properties went down by at least band. A total of 63,261 properties went up by two bands or more and this is about 5 per cent of the total properties in Wales (Welsh Government, 2005b).

Following the revaluation, the average band D CT bill rose from £887 in 2004/05 to £921 in 2005/06. This meant an average rise of £34 for properties that remained in band D. There was therefore a 3.8 per cent rise in average CT bills for a band D property following the revaluation. This rise was, in fact, the lowest annual percentage rise in CT bills for band D properties since CT was first introduced, for example, the 3.8 per cent rise in 2005/06 compared with 6 per cent in 2004/05 and 4.5 per cent in 2006/07 (StatsWales, 2016).

Reaction to the 2005 revaluation

This gap between expectations and reality mattered because it shaped the public and political reaction to the 2005 revaluation. Debates about revaluation were dominated by focusing on properties that moved bands and this had an effect on a further revaluation for Wales in 2015. Nick Bourne, the leader of the Conservatives in the Welsh Assembly, stated that 'Less than one in 10 households will benefit from going down a council tax band whereas more than a third will go up at least one band' (quoted in BBC News, 2005). The Chair of the WLGA, Alex Alridge, voiced similar concerns about the proportions of households moving up at least one band (Parry, 2005). Media coverage also described households that moved up bands as losers from reform. There was little discussion of those people who were possible winners either by dropping down bands or staying in the same band (Isaacs, 2005; Nifield, 2005; *Western Mail*, 2005).

The Welsh government responded to the worries over the revaluation by running a consultation in 2004 on a transitional relief scheme aimed at protecting households that moved up bands following the revaluation (Welsh Government, 2004c). Following this consultation, a transitional relief scheme was implemented which meant that no household could move up more than one band a year (Parry, 2005). On 2 November 2004, the Minister for Finance, Local Government and Public Services, Sue Essex (2004), announced that she was providing an extra £11 million for local government in 2005/06 to help fund the transitional relief scheme. The Welsh government records that the transitional relief scheme would run for three years (Welsh Government, 2005a).

Failed CT revaluation in 2015

The skewed nature of public debates over the CT revaluation was important as this then seemed to shape the fate of planned revaluations in England and Wales. On 3 December 2010, the UK Secretary of State for Communities and Local Government, Eric Pickles, announced that he was ruling out any CT revaluation in England during the 2010–15 Parliament because he was concerned about the impact of CT rises on family budgets. In doing so, he criticised the 2005 Welsh revaluation and argued that four times as many properties moved up bands than down (Department for Communities and Local Government, 2010).

Critics of the Welsh government alleged that Wales was a guinea pig for a potential CT revaluation in England. The critics argued that the UK government learnt from the 'mistakes' made during the 2005 revaluation. These mistakes included underestimating the losers from reform (*Western Mail*, 2005). In Wales, opposition politicians called for the planned CT revaluation in 2015 to be abandoned (Millar, 2010). On 9 December 2010, Labour First Minister of Wales Carwyn Jones and Plaid Cymru Deputy Prime Minister Ieuen Wyn Jones reported that they had asked the UK government to amend the Local Government Act 2003 to cancel the legal requirement to have the revaluation in 2015. Carwyn Jones cited UK government cuts to the Welsh government budget as a key reason why the Welsh government asked to be free of the need to revalue CT. He added that the estimated £5 million cost of a revaluation exercise would be better spent on protecting front-line services (see Williamson, 2009).

Discussion

What does the Welsh government revaluation of CT show about the feasibility of taxing wealth more heavily? During the revaluation process, the Welsh government paid attention to the winners and losers from reform. The Welsh government ruled out a shift from ninths to eighths that would have improved the progressivity of CT as this would have increased the losers from reform. Its transitional relief scheme was also aimed at cushioning the impact on the CT bills of properties that rose bands.

Nevertheless, a major limitation is that the Welsh government did not convey the complexity of reform adequately. The Welsh government devoted little attention to explaining the reform or informing the public how the winners from revaluation might also include properties that stayed in the same band after revaluation. Nearly three fifths of properties stayed in the same band after revaluation. Those properties that stayed in the same band might also be seen as winners. This is because their CT bills were arguably lower than they would have been with no revaluation.

The failure to communicate the complexity of reform meant that the Welsh government was put on the defensive in debates after the revaluation. Debates focused on the mismatch between the expectations and reality of those properties that moved between bands after the revaluation. It was easy for critics to portray the CT revaluation as a failed exercise. These worries were not just confined to the critics of reform, but also included its erstwhile supporters. The WLGA was one of the key backers of reform of CT and was involved in the reform process by taking part in the CTRWG. However, the WLGA voiced concern over the impact of revaluation on the movement of properties between bands. This skewed debates about CT reform in 2015.

Perhaps the main lesson from the Welsh CT revaluation in 2005 is that governments should take an active role in shaping how the winners and losers from reform are understood. Part of this may focus on highlighting the complexity of tax reform, which typically involves a varied set of winners and losers. Doing this might help rebut the arguments of critics that seek to present winners and losers in a particular way. Governments might also place more weight on developing arguments that challenge the framework of the tyranny of the status quo, as well as highlighting the complexities involved in using such a framework. The Welsh government did refer to arguments about fairness when outlining the case for reform in 2005. However, these arguments were dominated by the concern of the Welsh government to minimise the losers from reform.

Conclusion

Critics argue that financial inclusion has been used to support a neoliberal agenda. Perhaps the clearest example of this was covered in Chapter 4, which discussed housing. Critics allege that financial inclusion fostered a culture of borrowing to spend that led to a house price bubble. Chapter 4 claimed that it is possible to develop other models of financial inclusion that do not support a neoliberal agenda. The suggestion is that it is possible for financial inclusion to support an egalitarian agenda.

This claim invites a question about the likely outline of a more egalitarian version of financial inclusion. This chapter is an initial response to that question. The chapter has considered two influential agendas, namely, universal basic income and universal basic services. It looks at those policies as they seem the most obvious alternatives to financial inclusion. For example, universal basic services points to an extension of the welfare state. The chapter suggests that financial inclusion might be used to support both universal basic income and universal basic services. This chapter has also considered the feasibility of shaping such an alternative by examining the practicality of introducing egalitarian reforms. It has done this by looking at the case of one of the most challenging reforms, namely, increasing the taxation of wealth. The arguments in this chapter may be built on in various ways. However, the key claim made here is that financial inclusion can support a more egalitarian agenda.

6

Conclusion

Introduction

This book is about financial inclusion. This has been an explicit part of the social policy agenda since at least the 1990s. Even though some of the language around financial inclusion has gone in and out of fashion since then, the themes that underpin it have been an important part of social policy across many countries. Financial inclusion has been bound up with theoretical controversies or debates over financialisation. It has also led to policy developments within banking, insurance, savings and credit. Financial inclusion is an international agenda. It is an important part of the work of international organisations such as the World Bank and can be detected in national policy agendas. This book has paid particular attention to debates in the UK. A key reason for this is that the UK has been at the forefront of financialisation. Davis and Walsh (2017: 28) state that the 'UK was one of the earliest adopters of financialization and has one of the most financialized economies in the world'. The importance of financial inclusion is likely to grow rather than diminish in the future. Developments in financial technology and a move to a cashless economy may signal new topics for financial inclusion.

This section provides a brief summary of the argument of the book so far. Chapter 1 introduced the idea that there are two literatures that are largely developing in parallel to each other. One literature, much of it based on academic writing, is critical of financial inclusion and sees its aim as hollowing out the welfare state. A much more supportive position can be found in the policy literature and focuses on ways that boosting financial inclusion can reduce the costs faced by vulnerable groups of being excluded from financial services. Chapter 1 claimed that research would be enhanced if there is greater mixing of these literatures. Chapter 1 also suggested that it is possible to separate financialisation from neoliberalism. This is relevant because it opens up the possibility of shaping financial inclusion in different directions.

Chapter 2 argued that financial capability and financial inclusion are complementary. If people are to participate in the financial system, then they need to have the knowledge, skills and confidence to make financial decisions, as well as appropriate access to the financial system. However, the ideal mix between financial capability and financial inclusion is likely to vary in different areas. In some instances, the priority might be to boost financial capability, whereas in others, it may be more important to address access to the financial system. Furthermore, the mix between financial capability and financial inclusion may not be static and may change over time.

Financial inclusion aims to improve access to the financial system for all members of the population. An important part of the reality of everyday finance is that not all parts of the population have equal access to the financial system. This book has highlighted inequalities between men and women. For example, there is gender inequality within retirement pensions as pension systems have often been based on the contributions record of a full-time male worker in paid employment. One of the insights of feminist economics has been to reveal the unseen and unpaid caring work done by women in the household (Himmelweit, 2018). The gender inequality in pensions may also signal more general inequalities within the financial system. Women may face systematic inequalities in other areas besides pensions. Other groups in society also face disadvantages in the financial system, such as black and minority ethnic groups, people with disabilities, those on low incomes, and so on.

Financial inclusion policies might not erase all of these inequalities. Chapter 3 discussed the automatic enrolment into a workplace pension but noted that this initiative might worsen, not improve, gender inequality. AE ought to be adapted further so that it tackles the disadvantages faced by women. This points to a wider issue, namely, that financial inclusion policies may have varying effects across the population. This may mean that different policies are needed to improve financial inclusion for different parts of the population.

Chapter 4 claimed that it is important to embed the financial system within the wider economy. The book has paid particular attention to the case of housing given the close ties between the financial system and housing in one of the main public policy approaches adopted after the end of the Second World War. Further work in housing might examine different models of home-ownership and how these might be linked to the financial system. This is likely to involve examining shared or social ownership in greater depth. The relationship between housing and the financial system highlights that the financial system is part of the real economy. Further research might also examine the links between the financial system and other parts of the real economy. There is a need for more research that compares the merits of different policy options or alternatives. Any alternatives need to be feasible and this is likely to mean more research into the state and financialisation, and the different ways that the state may be needed to implement different policy ideas.

Chapter 5 considered some different alternatives for boosting income or wealth, such as a basic income or basic capital, as well as the feasibility of taxing wealth. This book has acknowledged that people need money if financial inclusion and financial capability are to have any real substance. Being connected to the mains is used as a metaphor for the importance of financial inclusion. However, this metaphor can be used to highlight the importance of money. For example, being connected to the electricity grid is important because it provides electricity. Similarly, being hooked up to the financial system is valuable because it is a conduit for money. Money – like electricity in the grid – is the lifeblood of financial inclusion.

No doubt some readers may prefer it if governments concentrate more on efforts to boost the income or wealth of people and households rather than encouraging people to make better financial decisions or widening access to financial services. If more money is spread across society and the economy, then the need for appropriate access to the financial system may increase. Therefore, the different agendas can be complementary. A redistributive agenda may be needed alongside financial inclusion to address economic inequality. This means attention being paid to taxes and benefits, alongside steps to support financial inclusion and capability. The challenge is not to ignore financial inclusion, but to find ways to make it work better.

What can critics learn from the supporters of financial inclusion?

This book claims that dialogue between the two literatures will advance research on financial inclusion. Much of this book has examined what supporters of financial inclusion might learn from its critics. It has suggested that a key way that this might occur is if supporters of financial inclusion engage with arguments about financialisation. For a genuine dialogue to occur, critics also have useful things to learn from supporters of financial inclusion. There are a number of possible things that critics might learn from supporters. One possibility draws on the level of policy detail that is often supplied by those sympathetic to financial inclusion. Government departments, think tanks, policy commissions and policy institutes are among the strongest advocates for financial inclusion. Often, the calls for financial inclusion contained in reports and so on make specific and detailed recommendations for policy. This policy detail can enhance theoretical discussions of financial inclusion.

Examining policy detail does not imply that critics should always have to engage with policy disputes. Critics should be free to pursue knowledge for its own sake and not be confined to studying only those areas tied to a specific social policy goal. However, as many critics of financial inclusion are already engaging with policy topics at some level, they might benefit from a deeper engagement with this literature. Nor does looking at the detail of policy mean that critique has to be abandoned. Rather, greater engagement might pave the way for more detailed criticisms.

The case of financial education in schools

This section looks at one example of what critics might learn from the policy literature. In particular, it examines the case of financial education in schools. Chapter 2 highlighted the importance of financial education as a way of building financial capability.

Financial education might be aimed at different parts of the population. For example, a range of different programmes might exist for those starting their first job, new parents, the self-employed or retirees. Financial education aimed at the young is a particular focus of policy activity. The Money & Pensions Service (2020: 10) identifies the young as a priority area for action: 'From our children, young people and parents research we are certain that we need to understand children's experience both in school and at home. So our measure covers children who get the benefit of a meaningful financial education in either a school or home environment.'

An investor-subject approach presents financial education as part of a project to create pliant financial subjects. Examining the young recognises that people can be moulded at a very early age, which highlights that the financial education of the young is worthy of attention. There are also practical reasons for paying attention to the financial education of the young. Any form of education requires 'teachable' moments or opportunities for learning. It may often be hard to identify such moments in practice. However, schools seem to offer a ready opportunity for mass financial education. This section looks at the UK as the UK is a leader in financial education. Financial education is developing in different ways in different parts of the UK and so this section sketches these different paths.

Financial education in England

Financial education became a statutory part of the national curriculum in England in 2014. Schools were required to teach financial education as part of the secondary school curriculum for pupils in key stages 3 and 4 (between ages 11 and 16). Pupils are required to study financial education as part of the curriculum for citizenship education and mathematics. The national curriculum guidance on citizenship education declares that students should have the skills to 'enable them to manage their money on day-to-day basis, and plan for future financial needs' (Department for Education, 2016: 227). The guidance on attainment levels states that key stage 3 pupils (aged between 11 and 14) should understand the role and use of money, the significance of budgeting, and how to manage risk. By key stage 4 (between ages 14 to 16), students should have an understanding of income and spending, savings, insurance, credit, different financial products and services, and how public revenues are raised and spent. Within the mathematics curriculum, pupils should be able to use mathematics to understand and solve problems in a financial context.

Financial education is not part of the primary school curriculum. However, there have been calls for financial education to be extended to cover the primary curriculum. In 2016, the All Party Parliamentary Group on Financial Education for Young People (2016: 7) underlined the role that schools play in the provision of financial education: 'Schools can, and do, play an important role in ensuring personal finance through effective financial education.' One of the main recommendations made is to strengthen the provision of financial education in schools. It calls for the Office for Standards in Education (Ofsted) to address how far schools are providing young people with financial education. It says that statutory financial education should be strengthened in the secondary curriculum by focusing more on real-life contexts. It also says that financial education should be part of the mathematics curriculum in primary schools. This report also suggests that financial education should be a key part of improving personal, health, social and economic (PSHE) education in schools.

Financial education in Wales

Financial education has been part of the school curriculum in Wales since 2008. It has therefore been part of the education system for longer in Wales than it has been in England. In 2014, the Welsh government asked Professor Graham Donaldson to review the school curriculum in Wales. The review proposed dividing the curriculum into six themes, namely: expressive arts; health and well-being; humanities; languages, literacy and communication; mathematics and numeracy; and science and technology. The Donaldson Review proposed that personal finance should be taught as part of the mathematics and numeracy area of study. Pupils would use personal finance as an area for applying mathematical and numerical skills (Donaldson, 2015).

The Donaldson Review was important for the Welsh government's revised school curriculum. In 2020, the Welsh government produced guidance for a new national curriculum that will come into effect from September 2022. Following the Donaldson Review, the curriculum will have six areas of study, namely: expressive arts; health and well-being; humanities; mathematics and numeracy; languages, literacy and communication; and science and technology. Financial education is presented within the mathematics and numeracy part of the curriculum. Financial literacy is embedded as part of teaching around the number system. Students are expected to understand the role that money plays as a type of exchange, and understand the value that notes and coins hold for payments. The guidance states that each student should be able to say: 'I can apply percentages and ratio to solve problems including simple and compound interest, appreciation and depreciation, calculating budgets, foreign currencies, and basic taxation on goods and services' (Welsh Government, 2020: 174).

Financial education in Scotland

The school curriculum in Scotland is known as the Curriculum for Excellence. This was introduced in 2010, following nearly a decade of debate. Curriculum for Excellence is aimed at children and young people aged between three and 18 years old. As with the Welsh government's school curriculum from 2022, the Curriculum for Excellence is split into different themes. There are eight areas, namely: numeracy and mathematics; sciences; expressive arts; social studies; languages; religious and moral education; technologies; and health and well-being (Kidner, 2013).

Financial education is part of the curriculum in numeracy and mathematics, as well as social studies. Within numeracy and mathematics, there is a section on 'number, money and measure'. The guidance on attainment outcomes notes that at an early age, pupils should be aware of how money is used, and in later years, should be able to understand the costs and risks of using bank cards to make purchases, and be able to use information on earnings and deductions to calculate net income. As part of social studies, students should understand the importance of budgeting and the different options for financing different types of business.

Financial education in Northern Ireland

A revised school curriculum in Northern Ireland was introduced in 2007. Guidance provided to teachers on financial capability states that the:

> Personal finance curriculum prepares pupils for their life as adults. Financially capable adults are able to make informed financial decisions. They are numerate and can budget and manage money effectively. They understand how to manage credit and debt. They are able to assess needs for insurance and protection. They can assess the different risk and return involved in different saving and investment options. They develop an understanding of the wider ethical, social, political and environmental dimensions of finances. (Council for the Curriculum, Examinations and Assessment, 2016: 4)

As with other parts of the UK, the main way that financial education is taught is through the mathematics and numeracy strand of the curriculum. In the primary curriculum, students are introduced to money as part of their studies of numbers. Pupils should be able to recognise different coins, as well as add and subtract money up to £10. Students should be able to discuss ways that money can be spent or saved, as well as alternatives to paying by cash. In the secondary curriculum, pupils discuss money as part of applying mathematical skills to everyday life. Suggested topics for teaching include discussing cash and non-cash methods for paying for goods or services, as well as the role of banks, building societies, credit unions and the Post Office in the economy (Council for the Curriculum, Examinations and Assessment, 2007a, 2007b).

Creating investor-subjects?

There are important differences in financial education policy in the UK. For example, financial education is part of both the primary and secondary curriculum in Wales but only the secondary curriculum in

England. A common theme of financial education across the UK is that it forms a part of the mathematics curriculum. Personal finance is a realm in which pupils can apply numerical calculations such as percentages or working out interest payments. An important part of the education also covers topics such as budgeting.

The capacity to make numerical calculations as well as understand concepts such as risk and return is compatible with an investor-subject approach. Investor-subjects ought to know how to budget properly as well as understand the likely returns from different types of investment. One might see financial education in schools, particularly at primary level, as part of an insidious effort to mould investor-subjects at a very early age.

However, financial education can also be used to support other agendas. Money is an important part of many, if not most, societies across the world. A capacity to make decisions about money is thus a significant part of everyday life. The concept of the everyday is becoming increasingly important in social policy research (McIntosh and Wright, 2019). There are many different types of financial system and so the nature of financial decisions will vary in different contexts. For example, the mix between the market, state and civil society differs in different countries. A common theme is that people and households have to make practical decisions about paying household bills, heating the home, buying things for children, travelling to work and so on. These are all examples of the everyday life of finance.

Understanding the role of money, budgeting, interest rates and how governments raise and spend money is likely to be important for any financial system. These types of knowledge are also useful for financial systems in which there is extensive welfare state provision. In England, financial education is also seen to be part of citizenship education. The aim of this citizenship education is to provide 'pupils with knowledge, skills and understanding to prepare them to play a full and active part of society ... [and] prepare pupils to take their place in society as responsible citizens, manage their money well and make sound financial decisions' (Department for Education, 2016: 227). Financial education might be genuinely aimed at building important skills for life rather than simply creating investor-subjects. Engaging more closely with the detail of policy may show that financial education is not tied necessarily to an investor-subject approach.

Although this book has noted the significance of financial capability, any problems in financial understanding may derive from organisations rather than individuals. Financial institutions might be the block to informed financial decisions. Financial institutions might overwhelm people with a mass of information that makes it difficult for people to make any decisions. Firms might also produce confusing or complex information that is difficult for people to understand. One response to this might focus on the idea of the responsible corporation (discussed later). However, the appropriate policy response might be to regulate the information provided to citizens rather than focus on individual skills. Rogers and Clarke (2016) highlight some of the challenges with regulation in their study of peer-to-peer lending in the UK. They say that several platforms (Funding Circle, Ratesetter and Zopa) accounted for nearly all peer-to-peer lending in 2011 and over half of market share (62 per cent) in 2016. Rogers and Clarke (2016) argue that the regulation of the peer-to-peer sector is an example of the capture of regulation by the regulated. These researchers claim that the regulations that have arisen have, in fact, yielded a notion of socially useful finance. This means that these platforms advanced socially useful finance by supporting lending for productive investments in the economy. They suggest that future research should examine how the regulation of socially useful finance might be established more formally.

Further areas of research

Financial technology

One strand of research that builds on the content of this book is to explore further the role of financial technology and the financial system. The spread of financial technology, or 'fintech', promises to have an important impact across all of the different fields of financial inclusion covered in this book. Fintech prompts interest as a low-cost delivery method that can have a very large reach across the population (Financial Inclusion Commission, 2015; Government Office for Science, 2015; Collard et al, 2016). Chapter 1 mentioned online banking and this is discussed further in the following. Financial technology might also be relevant for insurance, credit and financial capability. Financial technology might be used to allow people to buy more bespoke insurance products tailored to their needs. Crowdfunding sites such as Kickstarter also create the possibility that people will be able to access credit outside mainstream lenders.

Technology might also impact on financial capability by supporting the creation of online forums where people can share information or advice. This can be an opportunity for mutual education or learning. There is a growing body of work analysing the provision of advice on online forums (Pedersen and Smithson, 2013; Giles et al, 2015; Giles,

2016; Stanley et al, 2016; Montgomerie and Tepe-Belfrage, 2017). Montgomerie and Tepe-Belfrage (2017) provide an example of this when they analyse debt threads on three peer-to-peer Internet forums, namely, Mumsnet (a site aimed at parents, particularly mothers), Money Saving Expert (a personal finance website) and Consumer Action Group (which is a forum for individuals interested in challenging the charges made by banks). All three websites have important threads on debt. Montgomerie and Tepe-Belfrage (2017) claim that the analysis of these debt threads reveals the limits that the household economy places on financialisation. They argue that private debt is central to financialisation but that these debts need to be 'cared' for within the household. However, they note the ways in which debts can put households under strain and so undermine the conditions for its reproduction. This means that loans become non-performing, which spells catastrophe for neoliberalism.

Some scholars warn that financial technology might be used to advance neoliberalism. Montalban, Frigant and Jullien (2019) apply the methods of the 'French Regulation' School to analyse the platform economy. Montalban, Frigant and Jullien (2019: 807) define the 'platform economy as economic activities where tangible or intangible resources are exchanged between providers and users by the way of centralised electronic platforms'. They refer to the emergence of digital platforms such as Airbnb and Uber as examples of the new platform economy. The French Regulation School analyses the rules that govern the economy as a whole. This builds on an insight that all economies are embedded within a particular system of rules. Economies change when one set of regulations replaces another. Economies may be disembedded from a particular set of rules before resettling or re-embedding in a new context (Crouch, 2008, 2009; Van der Zwan, 2014; Montalban et al, 2019). Montalban, Frigant and Jullien (2019) suggest that the emergence of the new platform economy is best seen as a re-embedding of a neoliberal economy based around the digitisation of data. They claim that the 'platform economy has thus potentially deep connections with financialisation. It also accelerates previous neoliberal trends towards the flexibilization on the wage–labour nexus and outsourcing' (Montalban et al, 2019: 812).

Similarly, Gabor and Brooks (2017) argue that an alliance of international organisations and well-known philanthropists such as Bill and Melinda Gates support financial inclusion as a way of boosting development in low- and middle-income countries. Fintech is seen as a way of empowering local communities, building on policies such as 'microfinance'. Microfinance concerns locally based credit arrangements that allow local people to make investments to combat poverty. As noted in Chapter 1, mobile phones are seen as a way of reducing the unbanked in these countries. Gabor and Brooks (2017) signal the dangers with fintech when they argue that it might be used to create financial subjects. In particular, fintech might create data that are used to control people. They point to the:

> potential of digital technologies to capture the data of the newly 'included' in ways that enables lenders to map, know and govern 'risky' populations. In other words, rather than seeking to recognise people and things spatially in order to render societies 'legible' ... data generated via mobile technologies provide the means to 'administratively re-order' populations in new ways, based on the 'moving target' of behavioural data as opposed to more stable 'background' characteristics. (Gabor and Brooks, 2017: 430)

Although fintech might be a low-cost way of reducing some of the barriers that people face in accessing services, one should be alert to the ways that it might still extend neoliberalism.

The responsible corporation

Chapter 4 discussed the idea that Keynesianism and privatised Keynesianism are the two regimes that dominated policymaking in places such as the UK after the end of the Second World War. Colin Crouch, the author of the privatised Keynesianism thesis, claims that each of these policy regimes lasted for about 30 years before being beset by crises. For Keynesianism, this occurred in the 1970s during the period of stagflation that combined high unemployment and high inflation. For privatised Keynesianism, this became apparent during the 2008 global financial crisis. Crouch (2009: 394–5) writes that:

> Both Keynesianism and its privatised mutant each lasted 30 years. Given the rapidly changing character of capitalist economies, and the absence of any ultimate solution to their need to combine flexible labour and confident consumer, that probably counts as considerable durability. But the question arises: how are capitalism and democracy to be reconciled now?

Crouch (2009) suggests that the notion of the 'responsible corporation' is likely to be a key part of any new policy regime. He argues that there is a tension within neoliberalism over the part played by corporations within markets. Although neoliberal theory is committed to consumer sovereignty, much of the production in the market occurs through corporations. Companies introduce a tension within free markets because they allow the possibility of market power. One might add that the ambivalent role of corporations also mirrors a broader neglect within neoliberalism of collective institutions. For example, Montgomerie and Tepe-Belfrage (2017) argue that neoliberalism tends to treat the household simply as a 'black box' and ignores the way that relationships between men and women actually structure the household.

Crouch (2009) says that self-regulation is likely to unravel as corporate interests reassert their authority. He suggests that this would apply particularly to financial institutions: 'The dominant interests of contemporary society remain the great corporations, particularly those in the financial sector. They are currently suffering a loss of face, but both governments and mass prosperity depend on their efficient and lucrative functioning' (Crouch, 2009: 398).

In the decade since he wrote those words, Crouch (2020) has embarked on a research programme around 'post-democracy'. The general responsible corporation agenda is relevant for both theoretical and practical research into financial inclusion. First, corporate governance reform can shape the nature of financialisation. Van der Zwan (2014: 107) claims that a key part of 'financialization studies examines the ascendancy of the shareholder value orientation as a guiding principle of corporate behaviour'. She says that one sign of this is that financial markets put pressure on non-financial companies to maximise shareholder value. Berle and Means (1932) provide a classic account of the emergence of a shareholder model of the firm. During the 19th century, the owners of firms also managed most of their operations. As firms grew, there was a separation of ownership from control. The owners of firms delegated decisions about the workings of firms to a set of managers.

A shareholder approach insists that those people who buy shares are the rightful owners of a firm. Managers should then maximise shareholder interests, which is understood to mean the maximisation of profits and therefore share dividends. The separation of ownership from control gave rise to the 'principal–agent' problem, which focuses on how owners (principals) might guarantee that managers (agents) act in the best interests of shareholders. The principal–agent literature considers the different ways that it may be possible to align the interests of managers and shareholders, for example, by shaping executive pay:

> disciplining corporate managers through shareholder activism on the one hand, while creating a community of interest between managers and owners through the introduction of performance-based executive compensation on the other hand. In this financial conception of the firm, corporate efficiency is redefined as the ability to maximize individuals and keep stock prices high. (Van der Zwan, 2014: 107)

Van der Zwan (2014) sketches out how the shareholder value model has become increasingly important in different national contexts. Although different national institutions shape the content of this model, she says that the spread of the shareholder model contributes to the spread of financial markets throughout the economy and society. Although shareholder value maximisation has become increasingly important, it is not an immutable force. Van der Zwan (2014: 118) raises the possibility that it may be checked in various ways:

> In the context of weakening forms of interest mediation (labour unions, collective bargaining), associated with Fordism, new forms of political organization are likely to emerge. A number of scholars, for instance, have explored the cross-class alliances between workers and owners that have formed in the wake of the financialization process.

Van der Zwan (2014) focuses on the role that workers may play in resisting the spread of a shareholder value model. This draws on her analysis of firms, which presents managers, workers and shareholders as the key constituent parts of a firm. Although the role played by workers is important for alternatives to the shareholder value model, it is possible to extend this further to consider a 'stakeholder' model of the firm. Stakeholding is the subject of a large and growing literature (Rhenman, 1967; Freeman, 1984; Stoney and Winstanley, 2001; Laplume et al, 2008). Freeman (1984: 46) proposed that stakeholders are 'any group or individual who can affect or is affected by the achievement of the organization's objectives'. This is a very broad definition that admits a wide range of people or organisations. Indeed, one criticism of stakeholding is that this understanding can be stretched to almost anything as there may be limitless people or organisations that can affect, or be affected by, the aims of an organisation.

Laplume et al (2008) argue that five distinct themes can be seen in this literature on stakeholding. The first is the definition of stakeholder. Common examples of stakeholders include employees, consumers, supplier firms or local residents. The second is a discussion of the ways that stakeholders might influence firms, such as legal actions. The third is the actions of firms towards stakeholders, such as donations to charity. The fourth is the impact of stakeholding on the performance of firms. For example, supporters of stakeholding argue that it may be a way of boosting profits. The fifth is debates about the basis of stakeholder theory. Part of this covers normative or ethical arguments, such as the view that all stakeholders have moral worth because they should be viewed as an end in themselves.

Second, one might apply the preceding theoretical ideas to practical reforms of financial institutions. Ring (2012) argues that the behaviour of banks during the 2008 financial crisis undermined trust in financial institutions. Providing ownership stakes to citizens might be one route for rebuilding trust in financial institutions. For instance, mutuals are organisations that are owned by their members. There are different types of mutual that are relevant for financial services. Consumer mutuals give ownership rights to customers or users. Historically, building societies in the UK have given ownership rights to their depositors. Credit unions are bodies that also provide ownership rights to lenders. In the UK, these organisations do not form the majority of providers within financial services.

Mutuality might also be extended to cover other types of stakeholder, such as employees. One possible advantage of mutuals is that they might help address issues of trust in financial services. Customers may be more likely to trust those organisations in which they have some ownership stake. Managers might also be more inclined to take stakeholders into account if stakeholders have ownership rights in the organisation.

Public policy is likely to be important for creating the conditions needed for such diversity to arise. Laws and regulations are likely to be important for protecting certain types of organisational forms or allowing other types of organisation to emerge. Parkinson, Kelly and Gamble (2001) argue that the shareholder model of the company depends on being given a licence to operate by public authorities. The content of the licence to operate is therefore important for allowing a shareholder model to emerge and be sustained. In the UK, a wave of demutualisations of building societies occurred in the 1990s following changes in the law (Stephens, 2001; Cook et al, 2002).

Of course, mutuals might also have important limitations. It may be that mutuals have to be small in scale to allow for the interactions that are needed to build trust. If this is the case, then this would limit the extent to which mutuals could retain their benefits while also achieving mass scale within financial services. Empirical research will be needed to examine whether or not mutuality or stakeholding more generally does, in fact, boost trust in financial services compared to other types of organisation. Even if mutuals do enhance trust better than other organisations, other bodies might serve other valuable ends.

COVID-19 and future research

The Preface mentioned that this book was completed during the 2020 COVID-19 pandemic. The Office for Budget Responsibility (2020) published a scenario of the likely economic impact of the COVID-19 shock to the UK economy. Making a number of assumptions, it suggested that real national income would fall by about a third in the second quarter of 2020. Public sector net borrowing would rise to about 14 per cent of national income, which would be the highest annual deficit since the Second World War.

The responses to the economic and financial results of this crisis are likely to be an important area of research in the immediate future. The COVID-19 crisis promises to be as big a shock to the UK economy as the 2007–08 financial crisis. Long-standing supporters of a universal basic income, such as Guy Standing (2020), call for this policy to help people cope with the economic fallout of the pandemic. The pandemic has already prompted some sceptics to rethink their views on a universal basic income (Bush, 2020; Susskind, 2020a). COVID-19 presents the need for rapid and immediate relief. It may be very complex to devise rapid and targeted help, and so universal income payments have the virtue of simplicity.

However, emergency income payments might also be targeted at particular parts of the population. For example, Gustafsson (2020) reports survey data in May 2020 which suggests that 18–24 year olds (excluding students) were more likely than other age groups to have either been furloughed or lost their jobs because of COVID-19. One third of 18–24 year olds lost their jobs or were furloughed, and this is around ten percentage points higher than the next most badly hit age group (60–64 year olds). Henehan (2020) argues that experience from previous recessions such as the aftermath of the global financial crisis shows that the effects are most severe for those students that have recently left full-time education. This is also likely to be the case for the class of 2020 and COVID-19 (Henehan, 2020).

The class of 2020 will also be the first generation of 18 year olds in the UK to see their CTFs (or Junior ISAs) mature from September 2020. One possibility is that the UK government might place emergency deposits into these to address the special challenges that may be faced by the generation of 18 year olds coming of age in 2020.

Help might also be targeted at other parts of the population. Research suggests that the low paid are among those hit worst by the COVID-19 lockdown. In the UK, one third of employees in the bottom tenth of the earnings distribution work in sectors that were shut down during the lockdown period, compared with 5 per cent of those in the top tenth of the earnings distribution. Furthermore, women are more badly affected than men, with 17 per cent of female employees working in sectors that were shut down, compared to 13 per cent of male employees (Joyce and Xu, 2020).

Many households are facing falls in income but poorer households are less able to cope with drops in income because a larger part of their household budget is spent on essential items than richer households. On average, the poorest fifth of households spend around 55 per cent of their budgets on essential items, while the richest fifth spend around 39 per cent. This pattern is reversed for items that have been affected by social distancing measures, such as travel, leisure or eating out (Crawford et al, 2020). Poorer households may be in greater need of help than richer ones in coping with COVID-19.

One common objection to a universal basic income concerns the adequacy of this policy as a way of reducing poverty and inequality. Martinelli (2017b: 43, bold in original) summarises the nub of the issue when he states that the 'problem can be stated succinctly as follows: *an affordable UBI is inadequate, and an adequate UBI is unaffordable*'. This means that a universal basic income that is adequate to lift people out of poverty would be prohibitively expensive, while a policy that is deemed affordable would fail a test of adequacy.

The state has embarked on a staggering amount of public spending to safeguard the UK economy from COVID-19. Chancellor Rishi Sunak announced an initial package of support for businesses and households that amounted to £330 billion, or around 15 per cent of national income. At first sight, COVID-19 seems to have enlarged the realm of the possible for public spending. The immediate priority is to provide emergency help, and this has entailed mass state spending. One might claim that previous ideas about what is unaffordable no longer hold. According to this argument, the COVID-19 crisis has shown the extent to which government spending is driven by political choices. A universal basic income might therefore be deemed to be affordable.

One might counter, though, that it is very difficult to draw general lessons from the exceptional nature of COVID-19. Government spending here arose from a very specific set of conditions that, one hopes, are unlikely to be repeated for some time. The 2007–08 financial crisis ushered in a decade of austerity. A Conservative government charged with dealing with the aftermath of COVID-19 might make similar fiscal choices, and this is without taking account of the pressures on public finances from the UK's withdrawal from the European Union.

Some parts of universal basic services may also be useful in dealing with the fallout of COVID-19. Healthcare is an obvious priority. In the early stages of the crisis, the UK government moved fairly quickly to promise extra money for the NHS to help it cope with COVID-19. By mid-April, the UK government had also pledged around £15.5 billion of extra funding for the NHS to help it cope with COVID-19. Some aspects of a universal basic services approach are probably a greater priority at the moment than a universal basic income.

COVID-19 might also suggest that greater weight is now placed on information and access to the Internet. It became clear early on that there was a 'digital divide' faced by some vulnerable groups who could not access the Internet at home.

Schools were closed prior to the official lockdown. The education of schoolchildren depends largely upon them being able to access online lessons or homework from school. Evidence from the Lloyds Bank (2018) Consumer Digital Index shows that in 2018, 700,000 11 to 18 year olds (12 per cent) have no Internet access at home through a computer or tablet. Similarly, in the official lockdown period, employees who could work from home were instructed to do so. However, the capacity to work also depends on access to the Internet. Moreover, for the retired staying at home, the Internet is a way for them to maintain social contacts.

Similarly, the COVID-19 crisis promises important changes to how citizens access banking and payment services. The importance of these sectors was highlighted when the UK government designated them a key part of the economy during the lockdown (Cabinet Office and Department for Education, 2020). Physical distancing measures, which are likely to be in place for some time, mean that banks are encouraging greater use of online banking and UK government guidance is encouraging shops to use contactless payments wherever possible (HM Government, 2020).

This move to online banking and contactless payments may worsen the lives of the digitally left behind. An Office for National

Statistics (ONS) report notes that Internet use is an important part of the UK government's measures to achieve the UN's sustainable development goals (Serafino, 2019). However, 10 per cent of the UK adult population were classed as Internet non-users (have not used the Internet in the past three months). Almost half of adult Internet non-users are over 75 years of age. Women have consistently been over half of all Internet non-users. The Department for Environment, Food and Rural Affairs (2019) points out that rural areas have lower broadband speeds than urban areas.

Analysis by UK Finance (2019) reports that in 2017, debit card payments outstripped cash as the most popular payment method. Cash was still used in 28 per cent of all payments in 2018 and is projected to account for 9 per cent of payments in 2028. An Access to Cash Review (2018) states that poverty is the biggest indicator of dependency on cash. Those who pay by cash can expect to be increasingly excluded on the high street.

Behavioural theories, such as rational choice theory or behavioural economics, focus on individual capacities or preferences. ONS survey research from 2017 cites lack of digital skills as the second most common reason why people do not have the Internet at home (at 20 per cent). Common digital skills include: managing information; communication; transacting; problem solving; and completing online forms. Lack of interest (around 60 per cent) is the most popular reason for no Internet and this is particularly prevalent for older age groups (Serafino, 2019). However, people may encounter other barriers when accessing online banking or contactless payments. For example, the over-75s might also struggle with existing technologies as they need adapted or assisted technologies: 'technology in the future may enable the older age groups to engage more easily than is currently the case' (Serafino, 2019: 13). Addressing these forms of digital exclusion is likely to be important for reducing financial exclusion.

Conclusion

Financial inclusion is a varied and important area of research. This agenda has engaged scholars, policymakers and practitioners. This book has outlined some of the key debates in financial inclusion. It has also explored what this agenda means in policy, particularly in savings. Of course, the debate can be broadened by considering other policy areas not explored in this book, such as insurance. One of the main messages of this book is a call for greater engagement between the critical and supportive literatures on financial inclusion. As set out in

Chapter 1, the different literatures are tending to develop in parallel to one another. This book is one contribution to this mutual engagement and will hopefully prompt further dialogue.

Another key message of this book is that it is possible to shape financial inclusion in different ways. Financial inclusion is often seen as part of a project to turn people from citizens into investor-subjects. This book claims that financial inclusion does not have to develop in this way. It suggests that financial inclusion might be used to support a more egalitarian agenda. Others may prefer other models of financial inclusion. The nature of dialogue suggests that debates are likely to be ongoing as well as admitting of different points of view.

References

Access to Cash Review (2018) 'Final report'. Available at: www.accesstocash.org.uk/media/1087/final-report-final-web.pdf (accessed 30 April 2020).

Ackerman, B. and Alstott, A. (1999) *The Stakeholder Society*, New Haven, CT: Yale University Press.

Ackerman, B. and Alstott, A. (2004) 'Why stakeholding?', *Politics & Society*, 32(1): 41–60.

Ackerman, B., Alstott, A. and Van Parijs, P. (eds) (2005) *Redesigning Distribution: Basic Income and Stakeholder Grants as Cornerstones for an Egalitarian Capitalism*, London: Verso.

Adam, S. and Browne, J. (2012) 'Reforming Council Tax Benefit'. Available at: www.ifs.org.uk/comms/comm123.pdf (accessed 4 June 2020).

All Party Parliamentary Group on Financial Education for Young People (2016) 'Financial education in schools: two years on – job done?'. Available at: www.young-enterprise.org.uk/wp-content/uploads/2019/02/APPG-on-Financial-Education-for-Young-People-Final-Report-May-2016.pdf (accessed 18 February 2020).

Altman, M. (2012) 'Implications of Behavioural Economics for Financial Literacy and Public Policy', *Journal of Socio-Economics*, 41(5): 677–90.

Anderloni, L., Bayot, B., Blendowski, P., Iwanicz-Drozdowska, M. and Kempson, E. (2008) *Financial Services Provision and Prevention of Financial Exclusion*, European Commission: Directorate-General for Employment, Social Affairs and Equal Opportunities.

Appleyard, L., Rowlingson, K. and Gardner, J. (2016) 'The variegated financialization of sub-prime credit markets', *Competition and Change*, 20(5): 297–313.

Atkinson, A.B. (2015) *Inequality: What Can Be Done?*, Cambridge, MA: Harvard University Press.

Atkinson, A.B. and Messy, F. (2012) *Measuring Financial Literacy: Results of the OECD/International Network on Financial Education (INFE) Pilot Study*, OECD Working Papers on Finance, Insurance and Private Pensions, No. 15, Paris: OECD Publishing.

Atkinson, A.B., McKay, S., Collard, S. and Kempson, E. (2007) 'Levels of financial capability in the UK', *Public Money and Management*, 27(1): 29–36.

Attansio, O.P., Banks, J. and Wakefield, M. (2005) 'The effectiveness of tax incentives to boost (retirement) saving: theoretical motivation and empirical evidence', *OECD Economic Studies*, 39: 145–72.

Balakrishnan, R., Elson, D. and Heintz, J. (2011) 'Financial regulation, capabilities and human rights in the US financial crisis: the case of housing', *Journal of Human Development and Capabilities*, 12(1): 153–68.

Bank of England (2019) 'Credit union annual statistics 2018'. Available at: www.bankofengland.co.uk/statistics/credit-union/2018/2018 (accessed 4 June 2020).

Barbour, R. (2007) *Doing Focus Groups*, London: Sage.

BBC News (2005) 'One in three face council tax rise'. Available at: http://news.bbc.co.uk/1/hi/wales/3615952.stm (accessed 4 June 2020).

Bentham, J., Bowman, A., de la Cuesta, M., Engelen, E., Ertürk, I., Folkman, P., Froud, J., Johal, S., Law, J., Leaver, A., Moran, M. and Williams, K. (2013) 'Manifesto for the foundational economy', CRESC Working Paper 131. Available at: http://hummedia.manchester.ac.uk/institutes/cresc/workingpapers/wp131.pdf (accessed 16 October 2019).

Bergmann, B.R. (2004) 'A Swedish-style welfare state or basic income: which should have priority?', *Politics & Society*, 32(1): 107–18.

Bergmann, B.R. (2008) 'Basic income grants or the welfare state: which better promotes gender equality?', *Basic Income Studies*, 3(3): 1–7.

Berle, A. and Means, G. (1932) *The Modern Corporation and Private Property*, New York: Macmillan.

Berlin, I. (1958) 'Two concepts of liberty'. Available at: http://berlin.wolf.ox.ac.uk/published_works/tcl/tcl-a.pdf (accessed 5 June 2020).

Berry, C. (2015) 'Citizenship in a financialised society: financial inclusion and the state before and after the crash', *Policy & Politics*, 43(4): 509–25.

Blair, T. (1998) *The Third Way: New Politics for a New Century*, London: Fabian Society.

Bloor, M., Frankland, J., Thomas, M. and Stewart, K. (2000) *Focus Groups in Social Research*, London: Sage.

Bovens, L. (2009) 'The ethics of nudge', in T. Grüne-Yanoff and S.O. Hansson (eds) *Preference Change: Approaches from Philosophy, Economics and Psychology*, London: Springer, pp 207–19.

Brüggen, E.C., Hogreve, J., Holmlund, M., Kabadayi, S. and Löfgren, M. (2017) 'Financial well-being: A conceptualization and research agenda', *Journal of Business Research*, 79(October): 228–37.

Burke, E. (1999 [1790]) *Reflections on the Revolution in France*, Oxford: Oxford University Press.

Bush, S. (2020) 'Covid-19 has changed my thinking on universal basic income'. Available at: www.newstatesman.com/politics/economy/2020/04/covid-19-universal-basic-income-benefits-welfare (accessed 27 April 2020).

Butler, D., Adonis, A. and Travers, T. (1994) *Failure in British Government: The Politics of the Poll Tax*, Oxford: Oxford University Press.

Bynner, J. and Despotidou, S. (2000) *Effect of Assets on Life Chances*, London: Centre for Longitudinal Studies.

Bynner, J. and Paxton, W. (eds) (2001) *The Asset-Effect*, London: Institute for Public Policy Research.

Cabinet Office and Department for Education (2020) 'Guidance for schools, childcare providers, colleges and local authorities in England on maintaining educational provision'. Available at: www.gov.uk/government/publications/coronavirus-covid-19-maintaining-educational-provision/guidance-for-schools-colleges-and-local-authorities-on-maintaining-educational-provision (accessed 3 April 2020).

Camerer, C.F. (2007), 'Neuroeconomics: using neuroscience to make economic predictions', *Economic Journal*, 117(519), C26–C42.

Camerer, C.F. and Loewenstein, G. (2004) 'Behavioral economics: past, present and future', in C.F. Camerer, G. Loewenstein and M. Rabin (eds) *Advances in Behavioral Economics*, Princeton, NJ: Princeton University Press, pp 1–51.

Camerer, C.F., Loewenstein, G. and Rabin, M. (eds) (2004) *Advances in Behavioral Economics*, Princeton, NJ: Princeton University Press.

Camerer, C.F., Loewenstein, G. and Prelec, D. (2005) 'Neuroeconomics: how neuroscience can inform economics', *Journal of Economic Literature*, 43(March). Available at: www.cmu.edu/dietrich/sds/docs/loewenstein/neuroeconomics.pdf (accessed 4 June 2020).

Caplovitz, D. (1963) *The Poor Pay More: Consumer Practices of Low Income Families*, New York: Free Press of Glencoe and Collier-Macmillan.

Chaney, P. (2004) 'The post-devolution equality agenda: the case of the Welsh government's statutory duty to promote equality of opportunity', *Policy & Politics*, 32(1): 63–77.

Chaney, P. (2009) 'Equal opportunities and human rights: the first decade of devolution in Wales. A report commissioned by the Equality and Human Rights Commission'. Available at: http://citeseerx.ist.psu.edu/viewdoc/download?doi=10.1.1.614.6218&rep=rep1&type=pdf (accessed 4 June 2020).

Child Poverty Action Group (2005) 'CPAG briefing on the Child Trust Fund'. Available at: www.revenuebenefits.org.uk/pdf/ctf_cpag_evidence_nov_2005.pdf (accessed 4 June 2020).

Choi, J.J., Laibson, D., Madrian, B.C. and Metrick, A. (2002) 'Defined contribution pensions: plan rules, participant decisions, and the path of least resistance', in J. Poterba (ed) *Tax Policy and the Economy*, Cambridge, MA: MIT Press, pp 67–113.

Choi, J.J., Laibson, D., Madrian, B.C. and Metrick, A. (2004) 'For better or for worse: default effects and 401(k) savings behavior', in D. Wise (ed) *Perspectives in the Economics of Aging*, Chicago, IL: Chicago University Press, pp 81–121.

Clarke, J., Coleman, E., Grant, C., Samek, L. and Stokes, L. (2018) 'Employers' pension provision survey 2017'. Available at: https://assets.publishing.service.gov.uk/government/uploads/system/uploads/attachment_data/file/717607/employers-pension-provision-survey-2017.pdf (accessed 19 November 2019).

Clery, E., Humphrey, A. and Bourne, T. (2009) 'Attitudes to pensions: the 2009 survey, Department for Work and Pensions, research report 701'. Available at: www.gov.uk/government/uploads/system/uploads/attachment_data/file/214476/rrep701.pdf (accessed 11 August 2020).

Cole, I., Green, S., McCarthy, L. and Pattison, B. (2015) 'The impact of the existing Right to Buy and the implications for the proposed extension of Right to Buy to housing associations'. Available at: www.parliament.uk/documents/commons-committees/communities-and-local-government/Full-Report-for-Select-Committee-141015final.pdf (accessed 4 June 2020).

Collard, S. (2007) 'Toward financial inclusion in the UK: progress and challenges', *Public Money and Management*, 27(1): 13–20.

Collard, S. (2013) 'Workplace pension reform: lessons from pension reform in Australia and New Zealand', *Social Policy & Society*, 12(1): 123–34.

Collard, S. and Moore, N. (2010) 'Review of international pension reform'. Available at: www.gov.uk/government/uploads/system/uploads/attachment_data/file/214434/rrep663.pdf (accessed 4 June 2020).

Collard, S., Coppack, M., Lowe, J. and Sarkar, S. (2016) 'Access to financial services in the UK'. Available at: www.fca.org.uk/publication/occasional-papers/occasional-paper-17.pdf (accessed 11 September 2019).

Commission for Financial Capability (2015) National strategy for financial capability. Available at: https://cffc-assets-prod.s3.ap-southeast-2.amazonaws.com/public/Uploads/National-Strategy/PDFs/92262d1e19/National-Strategy-for-Financial-Capability-June-2015.pdf (accessed 13 August 2020).

Competition and Markets Authority (2015) 'Payday lending market investigation. Final report'. Available at: https://assets.publishing.service.gov.uk/media/54ebb03bed915d0cf7000014/Payday_investigation_Final_report.pdf (accessed 4 June 2020).

Consultative Forum on Finance (2002) *Council Tax Revaluation Working Group*, Cardiff: Welsh government.

Cook, J., Deakin, D. and Hughes, A. (2002) 'Mutuality and corporate governance: the evolution of UK building societies following deregulation', *Journal of Corporate Law Studies*, 2(1): 110–38.

Coote, A., Kasliwal, P. and Percy, A. (2019) 'Universal basic services: theory and evidence. A literature review'. Available at: https://ubshub.files.wordpress.com/2019/05/ubs_report_online.pdf (accessed 26 July 2019).

Coppack, S. (2013) 'The everyday geographies of financialisation: impacts, subjects and alternatives', *Cambridge Journal of Regions, Economy and Society*, 6(3): 479–500.

Corfe, S. and Keohane, N. (2018) 'Measuring the poverty premium'. Available at: www.smf.co.uk/wp-content/uploads/2018/03/Measuring-the-Poverty-Premium.pdf (accessed 22 October 2019).

Council for the Curriculum, Examinations and Assessment (2007a) 'The statutory curriculum at Key Stage 3. Rationale and design'. Available at: https://ccea.org.uk/downloads/docs/ccea-asset/Curriculum/The%20Statutory%20Curriculum%20at%20Key%20Stage%203.pdf (accessed 25 February 2020).

Council for the Curriculum, Examinations and Assessment (2007b) 'The Northern Ireland curriculum. Primary'. Available at: www.nicurriculum.org.uk/docs/key_stages_1_and_2/northern_ireland_curriculum_primary.pdf (accessed 25 February 2020).

Council for the Curriculum, Examinations and Assessment (2016) 'Financial capability. Post-primary guidance'. Available at: www.nicurriculum.org.uk/curriculum_microsite/financial_capability/documents/ks3_4/FC_Guidance_Booklet_Web.pdf (accessed 25 February 2020).

Crawford, R., Disney, R. and Emmerson, C. (2012) *Do Up-Front Tax Incentives Affect Private Pension Saving in the United Kingdom*, Institute for Fiscal Studies Working Paper W12/05, London: Institute for Fiscal Studies.

Crawford, R., Davenport, A., Joyce, R. and Levell, P. (2020) 'Household spending and coronavirus'. Available at: www.ifs.org.uk/publications/14795 (accessed 24 April 2020).

Creedy, J., Gemmell, N. and Scobie, G. (2015) 'Pensions, savings and housing: a life-cycle framework with policy simulations', *Economic Modelling*, 46: 346–57.

Crouch, C. (2008) 'What will follow the demise of privatised Keynesianism?', *Political Quarterly*, 79(4): 476–87.

Crouch, C. (2009) 'Privatised Keynesianism: an unacknowledged policy regime', *British Journal of Politics and International Relations*, 11(3): 382–99.

Crouch, C. (2020) *Post-Democracy after the Crises*, Cambridge: Polity.

CTRWG (Council Tax Revaluation Working Group) (2002a) *First Meeting: Wednesday 22 May 2002*, Cardiff: Welsh Government.

CTRWG (2002b) *Second Meeting: Tuesday 18 June 2002*, Cardiff: Welsh Government.

CTRWG (2002c) *Wednesday Meeting: Wednesday 21 August 2002*, Cardiff: Welsh Government.

Cunliffe, J. and Errygers, G. (2003) 'Basic income? Basic capital!' Origins and issues of a debate', *Journal of Political Philosophy*, 11(1): 89–110.

Dagdeviren, H., Donoghue, M. and Promberger, M. (2016) 'Resilience, hardship and social conditions', *Journal of Social Policy*, 45(1): 1–20.

Davies, S., Finney, A. and Hartfree, Y. (2016) 'Paying to be poor: uncovering the scale and nature of the poverty premium'. Available at: www.bristol.ac.uk/media-library/sites/geography/pfrc/pfrc1615-poverty-premium-report.pdf (accessed 22 October 2019).

Davis, A. and Walsh, C. (2017) 'Distinguishing financialization from neoliberalism', *Theory, Culture & Society*, 34(5/6): 27–51.

Davis, A., Hirsch, D. and Padley, M. (2018) 'The Minimum Income Standard as a benchmark of a "participatory social minimum"', *Journal of Poverty and Social Justice*, 26(1): 19–34.

De Henau, J. (2017) 'Costing a feminist plan for a caring economy: the case of free universal childcare in the UK', in H. Bargawi, G. Cozzi and S. Himmelweit (eds) *Lives after Austerity: Gendered Impacts and Sustainable Alternatives for Europe*, London: Routledge, pp 168–88.

De Wispelaere, J. (2016a) 'Basic income in our time: improving political prospects through policy learning?', *Journal of Social Policy*, 45(4): 617–34.

De Wispelaere, J. (2016b) 'The struggle for strategy: on the politics of the basic income proposal', *Politics*, 36(2): 131–41.

Deeming, C. (2017) 'Defining minimum income (and living) standards in Europe: methodological issues and policy debates', *Social Policy and Society*, 16(1): 33–48.

Demirgüç-Kunt, A., Klapper, L., Singer, D., Ansar, S. and Hess, J. (2018) 'The Global Findex Database 2017, measuring financial inclusion and the fintech revolution', World Bank Group. Available at: https://openknowledge.worldbank.org/handle/10986/29510 (accessed 4 June 2020).

Department for Communities and Local Government (2010) 'Standing up for local taxpayers: Welsh council tax revaluation cancelled'. Available at: www.gov.uk/government/news/standing-up-for-local-taxpayers-welsh-council-tax-revaluation-cancelled (accessed 4 June 2020).

Department for Education (2016) 'The national curriculum in England. Framework document'. Available at: https://assets.publishing.service. gov.uk/government/uploads/system/uploads/attachment_data/file/ 381344/Master_final_national_curriculum_28_Nov.pdf (accessed 17 February 2020).

Department for Environment, Food and Rural Affairs (2019) 'Broadband'. Available at: https://assets.publishing.service.gov.uk/ government/uploads/system/uploads/attachment_data/file/787740/ Broadband_March_2019__2018_data_.pdf (accessed 30 April 2020).

Department for Work and Pensions (2013a) The single-tier pension: a simple foundation for saving. Available at: www.gov.uk/government/ uploads/system/uploads/attachment_data/file/181229/single-tier-pension.pdf (accessed 10 August 2020).

Department for Work and Pensions (2013b) Framework for the analysis of future pension incomes. Available at: www.gov.uk/government/ uploads/system/uploads/attachment_data/file/254321/framework-analysis-future-pensio-incomes.pdf (accessed 10 August 2020).

Department for Work and Pensions (2013c) Automatic enrolment: qualitative research with large employers. Available at: www.gov.uk/ government/uploads/system/uploads/attachment_data/file/254182/ research-report-851.pdf (accessed 11 August 2020).

Department for Work and Pensions (2014a) Automatic enrolment: guidance for employers on certifying defined benefit and hybrid pension schemes. Available at: www.gov.uk/government/ uploads/system/uploads/attachment_data/file/307074/auto-enrol-guid-emp.pdf (accessed 11 August 2020).

Department for Work and Pensions (2014b) Automatic enrolment: experiences of workers who have opted out. Available at: www.gov. uk/government/uploads/system/uploads/attachment_data/file/ 288530/rrep862.pdf (accessed 11 August 2020).

Department for Work and Pensions (2014c) Automatic enrolment opt out rates: findings from qualitative research with employers staging in 2014. Available at: www.gov.uk/government/uploads/system/uploads/attachment_data/file/369572/research-report-9-opt-out.pdf (accessed 11 August 2020).

Department for Work and Pensions (2014d) Employers' pension provision survey 2013. Available at: www.gov.uk/government/uploads/system/uploads/attachment_data/file/330512/rr881-employers-pension-provision-survey-2013.pdf (accessed 11 August 2020).

Department for Work and Pensions (2015a) Workplace pensions: update of analysis on automatic enrolment. Available at: www.gov.uk/government/uploads/system/uploads/attachment_data/file/460867/workplace-pensions-update-analysis-auto-enrolment.pdf (accessed 14 August 2020).

Department for Work and Pensions (2015b) Automatic enrolment: qualitative research with employers staging in 2014. Available at: www.gov.uk/government/uploads/system/uploads/attachment_data/file/391153/rr899-automatic-enrolment-employers-2014.pdf (accessed 11 August 2020).

Department for Work and Pensions (2017) Automatic enrolment review 2017: maintaining the momentum. Available at: www.gov.uk/government/uploads/system/uploads/attachment_data/file/668971/automatic-enrolment-review-2017-maintaining-the-momentum.PDF (accessed 4 June 2020).

Dessimirova, D. and Bustamante, M.A. (2019) 'The gender gap in pensions in the EU'. Available at: www.europarl.europa.eu/RegData/etudes/BRIE/2019/631033/IPOL_BRI(2019)631033_EN.pdf (accessed 13 November 2019).

Disney, R. and Luo, G. (2017) 'The Right to Buy public housing in Britain: a welfare analysis', *Journal of Housing Economics*, 35: 51–68.

Dobbie, L. and Gillespie, M. (2010) *The Health Benefits of Financial Inclusion: A Literature Review. Report for NHS Greater Glasgow and Clyde*, Glasgow: Glasgow Caledonian University and Scottish Poverty Information Unit. Available at: www.gcu.ac.uk/media/gcalwebv2/theuniversity/centresprojects/spiu/Health%20Benefits%20of%20FI%20final%20report%20pdf.pdf (accessed 4 June 2020).

Dolan, P., Hallsworth, M., Halpern, D., King, D. and Vlaev, I. (2010) 'Mindspace. Influencing behaviour through public policy'. Available at: www.instituteforgovernment.org.uk/sites/default/files/publications/MINDSPACE.pdf (accessed 5 June 2020).

Doling, J. and Ronald, R. (2010a) 'Home ownership and asset-based welfare', *Journal of Housing and the Built Environment*, 25(2): 165–73.

Doling, J. and Ronald, R. (2010b) 'Property-based welfare and European homeowners: how would housing perform as a pension?', *Journal of Housing and the Built Environment*, 25(2): 227–41.

Donaldson, G. (2015) 'Successful futures. Independent review of curriculum and assessment arrangements in Wales'. Available at: file:///C:/Users/User/Downloads/Donaldson%20Report%20-%20Successful%20Futures%20-%20Independent%20Review%20of%20Curriculum%20and%20Assessment%20Arrangements%20in%20Wales%20(1).pdf (accessed 19 February 2020).

Donoghue, M. and Edmiston, D. (2020) 'Gritty citizens? Exploring the logic and limits of resilience in UK social policy during times of socio-material insecurity', *Critical Social Policy*, 20(1): 7–29.

Downes, A. and Lansley, S. (eds) (2018) *It's Basic Income. The Global Debate*, Bristol: Policy Press.

Drakeford, M. (2005) 'Wales and a third term of New Labour: devolution and the development of difference', *Critical Social Policy*, 25(4): 497–506.

Drakeford, M. (2007) 'Social justice in a devolved Wales', *Benefits: A Journal of Poverty and Social Justice*, 15(2): 171–8.

Dworkin, R. (1981) 'What is equality? Part 2: equality of resources', *Philosophy and Public Affairs*, 10(4): 283–345.

Edmonds, T. (2017) Financial inclusion (exclusion), Briefing Paper number 01397, 15 December, London: House of Commons. Available at: https://researchbriefings.parliament.uk/ResearchBriefing/Summary/SN03197 (accessed 14 August 2020).

Edmonds, T. (2018) Open banking: banking but not as we know it? House of Commons Library Briefing Paper. Available at: https://commonslibrary.parliament.uk/research-briefings/cbp-8215/ (accessed 10 August 2020).

Edna, G., Gale, W.G. and Halderman, C. (2020) 'Careful or careless? Perspectives on the CARES Act'. Available at: www.brookings.edu/blog/up-front/2020/03/27/careful-or-careless-perspectives-on-the-cares-act/ (accessed 2 April 2020).

Edwards, L. (2001) 'Equity stakes, fair stakes?'. Available at: www.ippr.org/files/uploadedFiles/projects/equitystakes110901.pdf?noredirect=1 (accessed 4 June 2020).

Elsinga, M. (2017) 'Living in assets without limits: towards new principles for policies on housing', *Housing, Theory and Society*, 34(2): 146–50.

Emmerson, C. and Wakefield, M. (2001) *The Saving Gateway and the Child Trust Fund: Is Asset-Based Welfare 'Well Fair'?*, London: Institute for Fiscal Studies.

Essex, S. (2004) *Cabinet Written Statement. Provisional Local Government Revenue and Capital Settlements 2005–06, 2 November*, Cardiff: Welsh Government.

European Commission (2014) 'Council recommendation on the United Kingdom's 2014 national reform programme'. Available at: http://ec.europa.eu/europe2020/pdf/csr2014/csr2014_uk_en.pdf (accessed 4 June 2020).

European Union (2015a) 'Directive (EU) 2015/2366 of the European Parliament and of the Council of 25 November 2015 on payment services in the internal market'. Available at: https://eur-lex.europa.eu/legal-content/EN/TXT/PDF/?uri=CELEX:32015L2366&from=EN (accessed 4 June 2020).

European Union (2015b) 'Revised rules for payment services in the EU'. Available at: https://eur-lex.europa.eu/legal-content/EN/TXT/HTML/?uri=LEGISSUM:2404020302_1&from=EN (accessed 4 June 2020).

European Union (2017) 'Bank accounts in the EU'. Available at: https://europa.eu/youreurope/citizens/consumers/financial-products-and-services/bank-accounts-eu/index_en.htm (accessed 4 June 2020).

Eurostat (2019) 'SDG 5 – gender equality. Statistics explained'. Available at: https://ec.europa.eu/eurostat/statistics-explained/pdfscache/63333.pdf (accessed 13 November 2019).

Feldman, G. (2018) 'Saving from poverty: a critical review of Individual Development Accounts', *Critical Social Policy*, 38(2): 181–200.

Fernandez, R. and Aalbers, M.A. (2017) 'Housing and capital in the twenty-first century: realigning housing studies and political economy', *Housing, Theory and Society*, 34(2): 151–8.

Ferran, E. (2012) 'Regulatory lessons from the payment protection insurance mis-selling scandal in the UK', *European Business Organization Law Review*, 13(2): 247–70.

Financial Inclusion Commission (2015) 'Financial inclusion. Improving the financial health of the nation'. Available at: www.financialinclusioncommission.org.uk/pdfs/fic_report_2015.pdf (accessed 4 June 2020).

Financial Inclusion Taskforce (2011) 'Financial Inclusion Taskforce research programme 2005–2011'. Available at: https://webarchive. nationalarchives.gov.uk/20130103022051/http://www.hm-treasury. gov.uk/d/fitf__research_programme_2005_2011.pdf (accessed 4 June 2020).

Financial Investor Education Foundation (2019) 'Investors in the United States. A report of the national financial capability study'. Available at: www.usfinancialcapability.org/downloads/NFCS_2018_ Inv_Survey_Full_Report.pdf (accessed 13 August 2020).

Financial Services Authority (2003) 'Towards a national strategy for financial capability'. Available at: https://webarchive.nationalarchives. gov.uk/20090414185718/http://www.fsa.gov.uk/pubs/other/ financial_capability.pdf (accessed 5 June 2020).

Financial Services Authority (2006) 'Financial capability in the UK: establishing a baseline'. Available at: https://webarchive. nationalarchives.gov.uk/20090704002653/http://www.fsa.gov.uk/ pubs/other/fincap_baseline.pdf (accessed 5 June 2020).

Finlayson, A. (2008) 'Characterizing New Labour: the case of the Child Trust Fund', *Public Administration*, 86(1): 95–110.

Finlayson, A. (2009) 'Financialisation, financial literacy and asset-based welfare', *British Journal of Politics and International Relations*, 11(3): 400–21.

Fitzpatrick, T. (2011) 'Social paternalism and basic income', *Policy & Politics*, 39(1): 83–100.

Fornero, E. and Monticone, C. (2011) 'Financial literacy and pension plan participation in Italy', *Journal of Pension Economics and Finance*, 10(4): 547–64.

Foster, L. (2012) '"I might not live that long!" A study of young women's pension planning in the UK', *Social Policy and Administration*, 46(7): 769–87.

Foster, L. (2017) 'Young people and attitudes towards pension planning', *Social Policy and Society*, 16(1): 65–80.

Foucault, M. (2007) *Security, Territory, Population: Lectures at the Collège de France, 1977–1978*, New York: Picador.

Foundation Economy Collective (2018) *Foundational Economy: The Infrastructure of Everyday Life*, Manchester: Manchester University Press.

Fox O'Mahony, L. and Overton, L. (2015) 'Asset-based welfare, equity release and the meaning of the owned home', *Housing Studies*, 30(3): 392–412.

Freeman, R.E. (1984) *Strategic Management: A Stakeholder Approach*, Boston, MA: Pitman.

French, S., Leyshon, A. and Wainwright, T. (2011) 'Financializing space, spacing financialisation', *Progress in Human Geography*, 35(6): 798–819.

Friedman, M. (1962) *Capitalism and Freedom*, Chicago, IL: University of Chicago Press.

Froud, J., Johal, S., Montgomerie, J. and Williams, K. (2010) 'Escaping the tyranny of earned income? The failure of finance as social innovation', *New Political Economy*, 15(1): 147–64.

Gabor, D. and Brooks, S. (2017) 'The digital revolution in financial inclusion: international development in the fintech era', *New Political Economy*, 22(4): 423–36.

Gamble, A. and Kelly, G. (1996) 'The new politics of ownership', *New Left Review*, 220 (Nov/Dec): 62–97.

Garratt, R.J., Mahadeva, L. and Svirydzenka, K. (2014) 'The great entanglement: the contagious capacity of the international banking network just before the 2008 crisis', *Journal of Banking & Finance*, 49: 367–85.

GfK NOP Social Research (2010) *Research on the Motivations and Barriers to Becoming 'Banked'*, London: Financial Inclusion Taskforce.

Giddens, A. (1998) *The Third Way: The Renewal of Social Democracy*, Cambridge: Polity.

Giles, D.C. (2016) 'Observing real-world groups in the virtual field: the analysis of online discussion', *British Journal of Social Psychology*, 55: 484–98.

Giles, D.C., Stommel, W., Paulus, T., Lester, J. and Reed, D. (2015) 'Microanalysis of online data: the methodological development of "digital CA"', *Discourse, Context and Media*, 7(1): 45–51.

Ginn, J. and Arber, S. (2002) 'Degrees of freedom: do graduate women escape the motherhood gap in pensions?', *Sociological Research Online*, 7(2). Available at: www.socresonline.org.uk/7/2/ginn_arber.html (accessed 4 June 2020).

Ginn, J. and MacIntyre, K. (2013) 'UK pension reforms: is gender still an issue?', *Social Policy and Society*, 12(1): 91–103.

Gómez-Barroso, J.L. and Marbán-Flores, R. (2013) 'Basic financial services: a new service of general economic interest', *Journal of European Social Policy*, 23(3): 332–9.

Gough, I. (2016) 'Potential benefits and pitfalls of a universal basic income', *The Guardian*, 10 June. Available at: www.theguardian.com/politics/2016/jun/10/potential-benefits-and-pitfalls-of-a-universal-basic-income (accessed 4 June 2020).

Gough, I. (2019) 'Universal basic services: a theoretical and moral framework', *Political Quarterly*, 90(3): 534–42.

Government Office for Science (2015) 'FinTech futures. The UK as a world leader in financial technologies. A report by the UK Government Chief Scientific Adviser'. Available at: https://assets. publishing.service.gov.uk/government/uploads/system/uploads/ attachment_data/file/413095/gs-15-3-fintech-futures.pdf (accessed 11 September 2019).

Gov.UK (2017) 'Parliamentary Under Secretary of State (Minister for Pensions and Financial Inclusion'. Available at: www.gov. uk/government/ministers/parliamentary-under-secretary-of-state--80#:~:text=Guy%20Opperman%20was%20appointed%20 as,Pensions%20on%2014%20June%202017 (accessed 17 August 2020).

Gov.UK (2019) 'The new state pension'. Available at: www.gov.uk/ new-state-pension/what-youll-get (accessed 19 November 2019).

Government of Wales Act (1998) 'Government of Wales Act 1998'. Available at: www.legislation.gov.uk/ukpga/1998/38/contents (accessed 4 June 2020).

Government of Wales Act (2006) 'Government of Wales Act 2006'. Available at: www.legislation.gov.uk/ukpga/2006/32/contents (accessed 4 June 2020).

Grady, J. (2015) 'Gendering pensions: making women visible', *Gender, Work and Organization*, 22(5): 445–58.

Gregory, J. (2014) 'The search for an "asset-effect": what do we want from asset-based welfare?', *Critical Social Policy*, 34(4): 475–94.

Gregory, J. (2016) 'How not to be an egalitarian: the politics of homeownership and property-owning democracy', *International Journal of Housing Policy*, 16(3): 337–56.

Gregory, L. and Drakeford, M. (2011) 'Just another financial institution? Tensions in the future of credit unions in the United Kingdom', *Journal of Poverty and Social Justice*, 19(2): 117–29.

Gustafsson, M. (2020) 'Young workers in the coronavirus crisis. Findings from the Resolution Foundation's coronavirus survey'. Available at: www.resolutionfoundation.org/app/uploads/2020/ 05/Young-workers-in-the-coronavirus-crisis.pdf (accessed 26 May 2020).

Haagh, L. (2011) 'Basic income, social democracy and control over time', *Policy & Politics*, 39(1): 43–66.

Haagh, L. (2019) 'The political economy of governance capacity and institutional change: the case of basic income security reform in European welfare states', *Social Policy and Society*, 18(2): 243–63.

Hacker, J.S. (2008) *The Great Risk Shift: The New Economic Insecurity and the Decline of the American Dream*, Oxford: Oxford University Press.

Halmetoja, A., De Wispelaere, J. and Perkiö, J. (2018) 'A policy comet in Moominland? Basic income in the Finnish welfare state', *Social Policy and Society*, 18(2): 319–30.

Hatherley, S. (2011) 'Sustainable public spending: the choice between universalism and targeting'. Available at: https://senedd.wales/NAfW%20Documents/ki-024.pdf%20-%2003112011/ki-024-English.pdf (accessed 4 June 2020).

Hausman, D.M. and Welch, B. (2010) 'Debate: to nudge or not to nudge?', *Journal of Political Philosophy*, 18(1): 123–36.

Hayek, F.A. (2001 [1944]) *The Road to Serfdom*, Abingdon: Routledge.

Heinberg, A., Hung, A., Kapteyn, A., Lusardi, A., Samek, A.S. and Yoong, J. (2014) 'Five steps to planning success: experimental evidence from US households', *Oxford Review of Economic Policy*, 30(4): 697–724.

Henehan, K. (2020) 'Class of 2020. Education leavers in the current crisis'. Available at: www.resolutionfoundation.org/app/uploads/2020/05/Class-of-2020.pdf (accessed 27 May 2020).

Hick, R. (2012) 'The capability approach: insights for a new poverty focus', *Journal of Social Policy*, 41(2): 291–308.

Hickman, P. (2018) 'A flawed construct? Understanding and unpicking the concept of resilience in the context of economic hardship', *Social Policy and Society*, 17(3): 409–24.

Hills, J. (2012) 'Getting the measure of fuel poverty. Final report of the fuel poverty review'. Available at: www.gov.uk/government/uploads/system/uploads/attachment_data/file/48297/4662-getting-measure-fuel-pov-final-hills-rpt.pdf (accessed 4 June 2020).

Hills, J., Bastagli, F., Cowell, F., Glennerster, H., Karagiannaki, E. and McKnight, A. (eds) (2013) *Wealth in the UK: Distribution, Accumulation and Policy*, Oxford: Oxford University Press.

Himmelweit, S. (2018) 'Feminist economics: why all economists should be feminist economists', in L. Fischer, J. Hasell, J. Christopher Proctor, D. Uwakwe, Z. Ward-Perkins and C. Watson (eds) *Rethinking Economics: An Introduction to Pluralist Economics*, Abingdon: Routledge.

HM Government (2020) 'Working safely during COVID-19 in shops and branches'. Available at: https://assets.publishing.service.gov.uk/media/5eb9703de90e07082fa57ce0/working-safely-during-covid-19-shops-branches-v1.1-250520.pdf (accessed 26 May 2020).

HM Revenue and Customs (2011) 'Child Trust Fund statistics: detailed distributional analysis of accounts'. Available at: https://webarchive.nationalarchives.gov.uk/20131006091359/http://www.hmrc.gov.uk///ctf/dda-2012.pdf (accessed 4 June 2020).

HM Treasury (1999) 'Accessing financial services. Report of PAT 14'. Available at: http://webarchive.nationalarchives.gov.uk/20130128101412/http://www.cabinetoffice.gov.uk/media/cabinetoffice/social_exclusion_task_force/assets/publications_1997_to_2006/pat_report_14.pdf (accessed 4 June 2020).

HM Treasury (2001a) 'Saving and assets for all. The modernisation of Britain's tax and benefit system, number eight'. Available at: http://webarchive.nationalarchives.gov.uk/20080814090308/http://hm-treasury.gov.uk/media/1/E/36.pdf (accessed 4 June 2020).

HM Treasury (2001b) 'Delivering saving and assets. The modernisation of Britain's tax and benefit system. Number 9'. Available at: http://webarchive.nationalarchives.gov.uk/20080814090308/http://hm-treasury.gov.uk/media/C/2/delivering_savings.pdf (accessed 4 June 2020).

HM Treasury (2002) *Pre Budget Report 2002: Steering a Steady Course. Delivering Stability, Enterprise and Fairness in an Uncertain World*, London: HM Treasury.

HM Treasury (2003) *Detailed Proposals for the Child Trust Fund*, London: HM Treasury and Inland Revenue.

HM Treasury (2004) 'Promoting financial inclusion'. Available at: http://webarchive.nationalarchives.gov.uk/20100104214853/http://hm-treasury.gov.uk/d/pbr04_profininc_complete_394.pdf (accessed 4 June 2020).

HM Treasury (2007) 'Financial inclusion: an action plan for 2008–2011'. Available at: http://webarchive.nationalarchives.gov.uk/20100104214853/http:/hm-treasury.gov.uk/d/financialinclusion_actionplan061207.pdf (accessed 4 June 2020).

HM Treasury (2010a) 'Budget 2010'. Available at: http://webarchive.nationalarchives.gov.uk/20130129110402/http://www.hm-treasury.gov.uk/d/junebudget_complete.pdf (accessed 4 June 2020).

HM Treasury (2013) 'Taskforce research'. Available at: http://webarchive.nationalarchives.gov.uk/20130129110402/http:/www.hm-treasury.gov.uk/fin_consumer_fininclusion_taskforce_research.htm (accessed 4 June 2020).

HM Treasury (2015a) Implementation of the EU payment accounts directive: consultation response. Available at: https://assets.publishing.service.gov.uk/government/uploads/system/uploads/attachment_data/file/477200/PAD_consultation_responses.pdf (accessed 14 August 2020).

HM Treasury (2015b) Spending review and autumn statement 2015. Available at: www.gov.uk/government/uploads/system/uploads/attachment_data/file/479749/52229_Blue_Book_PU1865_Web_Accessible.pdf (accessed 10 August 2020).

HM Treasury (2016) 'Budget 2016'. Available at: www.gov.uk/government/uploads/system/uploads/attachment_data/file/508193/HMT_Budget_2016_Web_Accessible.pdf (accessed 4 June 2020).

HM Treasury (2018a) 'Summary of Financial Inclusion Policy Forum meeting 19 March 2018'. Available at: www.gov.uk/government/publications/summary-of-financial-inclusion-policy-forum-meeting-march-2018/summary-of-financial-inclusion-policy-forum-meeting-19-march-2018 (accessed 16 December 2019).

HM Treasury (2018b) 'Summary of Financial Inclusion Policy Forum meeting 11 October 2018'. Available at: www.gov.uk/government/publications/summary-of-financial-inclusion-policy-forum-meeting-october-2018/summary-of-financial-inclusion-policy-forum-meeting-11-october-2018 (accessed 16 December 2019).

HM Treasury (2018c) 'Budget 2018'. Available at: https://assets.publishing.service.gov.uk/government/uploads/system/uploads/attachment_data/file/752202/Budget_2018_red_web.pdf (accessed 16 December 2019).

HM Treasury (2020) 'How to access government financial support if you or your business has been affected by COVID-19'. Available at: https://assets.publishing.service.gov.uk/government/uploads/system/uploads/attachment_data/file/873676/Covid-19_fact_sheet_18_March.pdf (accessed 23 March 2020).

HM Treasury and Department for Work and Pensions (2019) 'Financial inclusion report 2018–2019'. Available at: https://assets.publishing.service.gov.uk/government/uploads/system/uploads/attachment_data/file/789070/financial_inclusion_report_2018-19_web.pdf (accessed 16 December 2019).

HM Treasury and FCA (2016) 'Financial advice market review. Final report'. Available at: www.fca.org.uk/static/fca/documents/famr-final-report.pdf (accessed 14 August 2020).

HM Treasury and Glen, J. (2018) 'First meeting of the Financial Inclusion Policy Forum'. Available at: www.gov.uk/government/news/first-meeting-of-the-financial-inclusion-policy-forum (accessed 16 December 2019).

Hofman, A. and Aalbers, M.B. (2019) 'A finance- and real estate-driven regime in the United Kingdom', *Geoforum*, 100: 89–100.

Hogg, Q. (1947) *The Case for Conservatism*, West Drayton: Penguin.

Honoré, A.M. (1961) 'Ownership', in A.G. Guest (ed) *Oxford Essays in Jurisprudence*, Oxford: Oxford University Press, pp 107–47.

House of Commons Library (2009) 'Saving Gateway Accounts Bill'. Available at: https://commonslibrary.parliament.uk/research-briefings/rp09-02/ (accessed 4 June 2020).

House of Lords Science and Technology Select Committee (2011) 'Behaviour change'. Available at: https://publications.parliament.uk/pa/ld201012/ldselect/ldsctech/179/179.pdf (accessed 4 June 2020).

House of Lords Select Committee on Financial Exclusion (2017) 'Tackling financial exclusion: a country that works for everyone?'. Available at: www.publications.parliament.uk/pa/ld201617/ldselect/ldfinexcl/132/132.pdf (accessed 4 June 2020).

Independent Commission on Banking (2011) 'Final report recommendations'. Available at: https://webarchive.nationalarchives.gov.uk/20111108115104/http:/www.hm-treasury.gov.uk/d/ICB-Final-Report.pdf (accessed 5 June 2020).

Inland Revenue (2012) *KiwiSaver Evaluation: Opting-Out and Taking Contributions Holidays*. Wellington: Inland Revenue.

Inland Revenue (2015) 'KiwiSaver evaluation: Final summary report. A joint agency evaluation 2007–2014'. Available at: https://cffc-assets-prod.s3.ap-southeast-2.amazonaws.com/public/Uploads/2016-Review-Of-Retirement-Income-Policies/Making-Headlines/2ec1731bdb/129-Kiwisaver-IRD-KiwiSaver-evaluation-report-2015.pdf (accessed 11 August 2020).

Intergenerational Commission (2018) 'A new generational contract. The final report of the Intergenerational Commission'. Available at: www.intergencommission.org/wp-content/uploads/2018/05/A-New-Generational-Contract-Full-PDF.pdf (accessed 4 June 2020).

Isaacs, J. (2005) 'Raging about a tax issue', *South Wales Evening Post*, 7 July.

Jaime-Castillo, A.M. (2013) 'Public opinion and the reform of the pension systems in Europe: the influence of solidarity principles', *Journal of European Social Policy*, 23(4): 390–405.

Jayasuriya, K. (2000) 'Capability, freedom and the new social democracy', *Political Quarterly*, 71(3): 282–99.

John, P., Cotterill, S., Mosely, A., Richardson, L., Smith, G., Stoker, G. and Wales, C. (2011) *Nudge, Nudge, Think, Think: Experimenting with Ways to Change Civic Behaviour*, London: Bloomsbury Academic.

Johnson, E. and Sherraden, M.S. (2007) 'From financial literacy to financial capability among youth', *Journal of Sociology and Social Welfare*, 34(3): 119–45.

Johnson, P. and Myles, G. (2011) 'The Mirrlees Review', *Fiscal Studies*, 32(3): 319–29.

Jones, C. and Murie, A. (2006) *The Right to Buy: Analysis and Evaluation of a Housing Policy*, Oxford: Blackwell.

Jones, C., Leishman, C. and Orr, A.M. (2006a) 'The revaluation of council tax bands: more than rearranging the deck chairs', *Policy & Politics*, 34(2): 219–39.

Jones, C., Leishman, C. and Orr, A.M. (2006b) 'The potential impact of reforms to the essential parameters of the council tax', *Fiscal Studies*, 27(2): 205–29.

Jones, R., Pykett, J. and Whitehead, M. (2014) 'The geographies of policy translation: how nudge became the default policy option', *Environment and Planning C: Government and Policy*, 32: 54–69.

Jordà, Ò., Schularick, M. and Taylor, A.M. (2014) 'Betting the house', *Journal of International Economics*, 96: S2–S18.

Joyce, R. and Xu, X. (2020) 'Sector shut-downs during the coronavirus crisis affect the youngest and lowest paid workers, and women, the most'. Available at: www.ifs.org.uk/publications/14797 (accessed 27 April 2020).

Kahneman, D. (2011) *Thinking, Fast and Slow*, London: Penguin.

Kahneman, D. and Tversky, A. (1979) 'Prospect theory: an analysis of decision under risk', *Econometrica*, 47: 263–92.

Kaplow, L. (2011) 'An optimal tax system', *Fiscal Studies*, 32(3): 415–35.

Karimli, L., Ssewamala, F. and Neilands, T.B. (2014) 'Poor families striving to save in matched children's savings accounts: findings from a randomized experimental design in Uganda', *Social Service Review*, 88(4): 658–94.

Karwowski, E. (2019) 'Towards (de-)financialisation: the role of the state', *Cambridge Journal of Economics*, 43: 1001–27.

Kelly, G. and Lissauer, R. (2000) *Ownership for All*, London: Institute for Public Policy Research.

Kempson, E. (2009) 'Framework for the development of financial literacy baseline surveys: a first international comparative analysis', OECD Working Papers on Finance, Insurance and Private Pensions, No. 1, OECD Publishing.

Kempson, E. and Whyley, C. (1999) 'Kept in or opted out? Understanding and combating financial exclusion'. Available at: www.bristol.ac.uk/media-library/sites/geography/migrated/documents/pfrc9902.pdf (accessed 20 June 2019).

Kenway, P. and Palmer, G. (1999) *Council Tax: The Case for Reform*, London: New Policy Institute.

Kidner, C. (2013) 'Curriculum for excellence'. Available at: www. parliament.scot/ResearchBriefingsAndFactsheets/S4/SB_13-13.pdf (accessed 20 February 2020).

King, A. and Crewe, I. (2014) *The Blunders of Our Governments*, London: Oneworld.

Klapper, L. and Singer, D. (2014) 'The opportunities of digitizing payments. How digitization of payments, transfers and remittances contributes to the G20 goals of broad-based economic growth, financial inclusion and women's economic empowerment. Full report'. Available at: http://documents.worldbank.org/curated/en/188451468336589650/The-opportunities-of-digitizing-payments (accessed 4 June 2020).

Kotarski, K. and Brkic, L. (2017) 'Political economy of banking and debt crisis in the EU: rising financialization and its ramifications', *Review of Radical Political Economics*, 49(3): 430–55.

Lai, K.P.Y. (2017) 'Unpacking financial subjectivities: intimacies, governance and socioeconomic practices in financialisation', *Environment and Planning D: Society and Space*, 35(5): 913–32.

Langley, P. (2008) *The Everyday Life of Global Finance: Saving and Borrowing in Anglo-America*, Oxford: Oxford University Press.

Laplume, A.O., Sonpar, K. and Litz, R.A. (2008) 'Stakeholder theory: reviewing a theory that moves us', *Journal of Management*, 34(6): 1152–89.

Le Grand, J. and Nissan, D. (2000) *A Capital Idea: Start-Up Grants for Young People*, London: Fabian Society.

Lefebure, S., Mangeleer, J. and Van den Bosch, K. (2006) 'Elderly prosperity and homeownership in the European Union: new evidence from the SHARE data', paper presented to the 29th General Conference of the International Association for Research in Income and Wealth. Available at: www.iariw.org/papers/2006/lefebure.pdf (accessed 4 June 2020).

Lehto, O. (2018) 'Basic Income around the world. The unexpected benefits of unconditional cash transfers'. Available at: https://static1.squarespace.com/static/56eddde762cd9413e151ac92/t/5a5f54ff53450ae87509190a/1516197120863/Universal+Basic+Income.pdf (accessed 4 June 2020).

Lennartz, C. and Ronald, R. (2017) 'Asset-based welfare and social investment: competing, compatible, or complementary social policy strategies for the new welfare state?', *Housing, Theory and Society*, 34(2): 201–20.

Lewis, H. (2010a) *Deputy Minister Launches Cardigan Child Trust Fund Initiative*, 11 February, Cardiff: Welsh Government.

Lewis, H. (2010b) *Written Statement – Child Trust Funds*, 3 December, Cardiff: Welsh Government.

Leyshon, A. and Thrift, N. (1994) 'Access to financial services and financial infrastructure withdrawal: problems and policies', *Area*, 26(3): 268–75.

Leyshon, A. and Thrift, N. (1995) 'Geographies of financial exclusion: financial abandonment in Britain and the United States', *Transactions of the Institute of British Geographers*, 20(3): 312–41.

Leyshon, A., Burton, D., Knights, D., Aleroff, C. and Signoretta, P. (2004) 'Ecologies of retail financial services: understanding the persistence of door-to-door credit and insurance providers', *Environment and Planning A*, 36(4): 625–45.

Lister, R. (2003 [1997]) *Citizenship: Feminist Perspectives* (ed. J. Campling), Basingstoke: Palgrave-Macmillan.

Lister, R. and Sodha, S. (2016) 'The saving gateway: from principles to practice'. Available at: www.ippr.org/files/images/media/files/publication/2011/05/the_saving_gateway_full_1541.pdf (accessed 13 August 2020).

Lloyds Bank (2018) 'UK Consumer Digital Index'. Available at: www.lloydsbank.com/assets/media/pdfs/banking_with_us/whats-happening/LB-Consumer-Digital-Index-2018-Report.pdf (accessed 27 April 2020).

Loke, V. and Sacco, P. (2011) 'Changes in parental assets and children's educational outcomes', *Journal of Social Policy*, 40(2): 351–68.

Lowe, J. (2012) 'Pensions', in G. Callaghan, I. Fribbance and M. Higginson (eds) *Personal Finance*, Basingstoke: Palgrave MacMillan, pp 273–324.

Lowe, S.G., Searle, B.A. and Smith, S.J. (2011) 'From housing wealth to mortgage debt: the emergence of Britain's asset-shaped welfare state', *Social Policy and Society*, 11(1): 105–16.

Lund, B. (2013) 'A "property-owning democracy" or "generation rent"?', *Political Quarterly*, 84(1): 53–60.

Lusardi, A. (2019), 'Financial literacy and the need for financial education: evidence and implications', *Swiss Journal of Economics and Statistics*, 155(1): 1–8. Available at: https://sjes.springeropen.com/track/pdf/10.1186/s41937-019-0027-5 (accessed 13 August 2020).

Lusardi, A. and Mitchell, O. (2011) 'Financial literacy around the world: an overview', *Journal of Pension Economics and Finance*, 10(4): 497–508.

Lusardi, A. and Mitchell, O. (2014) 'The economic importance of financial literacy: theory and evidence', *Journal of Economic Literature*, 52(1): 5–44.

Lusardi, A., Samek, A.S., Kapteyn, A., Glinert, L., Hung, A. and Heinberg, A. (2017) 'Visual tools and narratives: new ways to improve financial literacy', *Journal of Pension Economics and Finance*, 16(3): 297–323.

Lyons, M. (2007) 'Lyons inquiry into local government'. Available at: www.webarchive.org.uk/wayback/archive/20070428120000/http://www.lyonsinquiry.org.uk/docs/final-complete.pdf (accessed 4 June 2020).

Maclennan, D. and Miao, J. (2017) 'Housing and capital in the 21st century', *Housing, Theory and Society*, 34(2): 127–45.

MacLeod, P., Fitzpatrick, A., Hamlyn, B., Jones, A., Kinver, A. and Page, L. (2012) Attitudes to pensions: the 2012 survey, Department for Work and Pensions, Research Report 813. Available at: www.gov.uk/government/uploads/system/uploads/attachment_data/file/193372/rrep813.pdf (accessed 11 August 2020).

Madrian, B.C. and Shea, D.F. (2001) 'The power of suggestion: inertia in 401(k) participation and savings behaviour', *Quarterly Journal of Economics*, 116: 1149–225.

Marquand, D. (1997) *The New Reckoning*, Cambridge: Polity.

Marron, D. (2013) 'Governing poverty in a neoliberal age: New Labour and the case of financial exclusion', *New Political Economy*, 18(6): 785–810.

Marron, D. (2014) ' "Informed, educated and more confident": financial capability and the problematization of personal finance consumption', *Consumption, Markets & Culture*, 17(5): 491–511.

Marshall, T.H. (1950) *Citizenship and Social Class and Other Essays*, Cambridge: Cambridge University Press.

Martinelli, L. (2017a) 'The fiscal and distributional implications of alternative universal basic income schemes in the UK'. Available at: www.bath.ac.uk/publications/the-fiscal-and-distributional-implications-of-alternative-universal-basic-income-schemes-in-the-uk/attachments/Basic_Income_Working_Paper.pdf (accessed 4 June 2020).

Martinelli, L. (2017b) 'Assessing the case for a universal basic income in the UK'. Available at: www.bath.ac.uk/publications/assessing-the-case-for-a-universal-basic-income-in-the-uk/attachments/basic_income_policy_brief.pdf (accessed 4 June 2020).

McIntosh, I. and Wright, S. (2019) 'Exploring what the notion of "lived experience" offers for social policy analysis', *Journal of Social Policy*, 48(3): 449–67.

McKay, S., Rowlingson, K. and Overton, L. (2019) 'Financial inclusion annual monitoring briefing paper 2019'. Available at: www.birmingham.ac.uk/Documents/college-social-sciences/social-policy/CHASM/financial-inclusion/19003-Financial-inclusion-2019-Briefing-Paper-AWLR.pdf (accessed 23 October 2019).

McKernan, S.-M. and Sherraden, M. (eds) (2008) *Asset Building and Low-Income Families*, Washington, DC: Urban Institute Press.

McKillop, D. and Wilson, J. (2008) *Credit Unions in Scotland*, Edinburgh: Scottish Government. Available at: www.researchgate.net/publication/255624090_CREDIT_UNIONS_IN_SCOTLAND (accessed 5 June 2020).

McKillop, D., Ward, A.M. and Wilson, J. (2011) 'Credit unions in Great Britain: recent trends and current prospects', *Public Money and Management*, 31: 35–42.

McQuaid, R. and Egdell, V. (2010) 'Financial capability – evidence review'. Available at: www.scotland.gov.uk/Resource/Doc/304557/0102282.pdf (accessed 4 June 2020).

Meade, J.E. (1964) *Efficiency, Equality and the Ownership of Property*, London: George Allen and Unwin.

Millar, D. (2010) 'Supporting businesses and householders'. Available at: www.conservatives.wales/news/darren-millar-supporting-businesses-and-householders (accessed 4 June 2020).

Mirrlees, J., Adam, S., Besley, T., Blundell, R., Bond, S., Chote, R., Gammie, M., Johnson, P., Myles, G. and Poterba, J. (2011a) 'The taxation of land and property', in J. Mirrlees, S. Adam, T. Besley, R. Blundell, S. Bond, R. Chote, M. Gammie, P. Johnson, G. Myles and J. Poterba (eds) *Tax by Design: The Mirrlees Review*, London: Institute for Fiscal Studies. Available at: www.ifs.org.uk/publications/5353 (accessed 4 June 2020).

Mirrlees, J., Adam, S., Besley, T., Blundell, R., Bond, S., Chote, R., Gammie, M., Johnson, P., Myles, G. and Poterba, J. (2011b) 'Tax by design: the Mirrlees Review. Conclusions and recommendations for reform'. Available at: www.ifs.org.uk/publications/5353 (accessed 4 June 2020).

Mitton, L. (2008) 'Financial inclusion in the UK: review of policy and practice'. Available at: www.jrf.org.uk/report/financial-inclusion-uk-review-policy-and-practice (accessed 4 June 2020).

Money Advice Service (2015a) 'Financial capability in the UK 2015. Initial results from the 2015 UK Financial Capability Survey'. Available at: https://prismic-io.s3.amazonaws.com/fincap-two%2Fd08746d1-e667-4c9e-84ad-8539ce5c62e0_mas_fincap_uk_survey_2015_aw.pdf (accessed 4 June 2020).

Money Advice Service (2015b) 'Financial capability. Strategy for the UK'. Available at: https://prismic-io.s3.amazonaws.com/fincap-two%2F98a4b453-cc74-48d0-a301-8c5274adc389_uk+financial+capability+strategy.pdf (accessed 4 June 2020).

Money Advice Service (2018) 'Building the financial capability of UK adults. Initial findings from 2018 Adult Financial Capability Survey'. Available at: www.fincap.org.uk/en/articles/financial-capability-survey (accessed 5 August 2019).

Money & Pensions Service (2020) 'The UK strategy for financial wellbeing'. Available at: www.maps.org.uk/wp-content/uploads/2020/01/UK-Strategy-for-Financial-Wellbeing-2020-2030-Money-and-Pensions-Service.pdf (accessed 17 February 2020).

Montalban, M., Figant, V. and Jullien, B. (2019) 'Platform economy as a new form of capitalism: a *régulationist* research programme', *Cambridge Journal of Economics*, 43: 805–24.

Montgomerie, J. (2008) 'Bridging the critical divide: global finance, financialisation and contemporary capitalism', *Contemporary Politics*, 14(3): 233–52.

Montgomerie, J. and Büdenbender, M. (2015) 'Round the houses: homeownership and failures of asset-based welfare in the United Kingdom', *New Political Economy*, 20(3): 386–405.

Montgomerie, J. and Tepe-Belfrage, D. (2017) 'Caring for debts: how the household economy exposes the limits of financialisation', *Critical Sociology*, 43(4/5): 653–68.

Mooney, G. and Williams, C. (2006) ' "Forging new ways of life"? Social policy and nation building in devolved Scotland and Wales', *Critical Social Policy*, 26(3): 608–29.

More, T. (2020 [1516]) *Utopia*, London: Penguin.

Morgan, K. and Price, A. (2011) *The Collective Entrepreneur: Social Enterprise and the Smart State*, Cardiff: Charity Bank and Community Housing Cymru.

Morgan, R. (2002) 'Clear red water', speech at the National Centre for Public Policy, Swansea, 11 December. Available at: www.sochealth.co.uk/Regions/Wales/redwater.htm (accessed 4 June 2020).

Morgan, R. (2006) 'Rhodri Morgan outlines a Welsh recipe for 21st century socialism at packed Compass meeting in Swansea', 1 December.

Muellbauer, J. and Cameron, G. (2000) 'Five key council tax reforms', *New Economy*, 7(2): 88–91.

Muir, K., Marjolin, A. and Adams, S. (2015) 'Eight years on the fringe: what has it meant to be severely or fully financially excluded in Australia?', Centre for Social Impact for the National Australia Bank. Available at: www.csi.edu.au/media/uploads/Eight_Years_on_ the_Fringe_FINAL_FINAL.pdf (accessed 4 June 2020).

Nam, Y., Huang, J. and Sherraden, M. (2008) 'Asset definitions', in S.-M. McKernan and M. Sherraden (eds) *Asset Building and Low-Income Families*, Washington, DC: Urban Institute Press, pp 1–31.

Natali, D. (2018) 'Occupational pensions in Europe: Trojan horse of financialization?', *Social Policy and Administration*, 52(2): 449–62.

National Assembly for Wales (2000) 'Simplifying the system: local government finance in Wales. A consultation paper from the Cabinet of the National Assembly', Cardiff: National Assembly for Wales.

National Assembly for Wales (2011) 'Further powers. The referendum result explained'. Available at: www.assemblywales.org/yes_vote_ leaflet.pdf (accessed 4 June 2020).

National Employment Savings Trust Corporation (2015) National Employment Savings Trust Corporation annual report and accounts 2014–2015. Available at: www.gov.uk/government/uploads/system/ uploads/attachment_data/file/445692/nest-annual-report-and-accounts-2014-2015-2.pdf (accessed 11 August 2020).

National Strategy for Financial Literacy (2015), 'Count me in, Canada'. Available at: www.canada.ca/content/dam/canada/ financial-consumer-agency/migration/eng/financialliteracy/ financialliteracycanada/strategy/documents/nationalstrategyforfina ncialliteracycountmeincanada.pdf (accessed 13 August 2020).

Nifield, P. (2005) 'Re-banding guinea pig', *South Wales Echo*, 22 April.

Nussbaum, M. (2000) *Women and Human Development: The Capabilities Approach*, Cambridge: Cambridge University Press.

Nussbaum, M. (2011) *Creating Capabilities*, Cambridge, MA: Harvard University Press.

O'Donnell, N. and Keeney, M. (2010) 'Financial capability in Ireland and a comparison with the UK', *Public Money and Management*, 30(6): 355–62.

OECD (2016) 'OECD/INFE international survey of adult financial literacy competencies'. Available at: www.oecd.org/daf/fin/financial-education/OECD-INFE-International-Survey-of-Adult-Financial-Literacy-Competencies.pdf (accessed 9 December 2019).

OECD (2018) 'OECD/INFE toolkit for measuring financial literacy and financial inclusion'. Available at: www.oecd.org/daf/fin/ financial-education/2018-INFE-FinLit-Measurement-Toolkit.pdf (accessed 7 August 2019).

Office for Budget Responsibility (2020) 'Commentary on the OBR coronavirus reference scenario'. Available at: https://cdn.obr.uk/Coronavirus_reference_scenario_commentary.pdf (accessed 22 April 2020).

Olin Wright, E. (2004) 'Basic income, stakeholder grants and class analysis', *Politics & Society*, 32(1): 79–87.

Olin Wright, E. (2015) 'Eroding capitalism: a comment on Stuart White's "Basic capital in the egalitarian toolkit"', *Journal of Applied Philosophy*, 32(4): 432–9.

Oliver, A. (2013) 'From nudging to budging: using behavioural economics to inform public sector policy', *Journal of Social Policy*, 42(4): 685–700.

Oliver, A. (2015) 'Nudging, shoving, and budging: behavioural economic-informed policy', *Public Administration*, 93(3): 700–14.

Opinion Leader Research (2006) Financial inclusion deliberative workshops. Prepared for HM Treasury/Financial Inclusion Taskforce by Opinion Leader Research. Available at: http://webarchive.nationalarchives.gov.uk/20100104214853/http://hm-treasury.gov.uk/d/opinion_leader_deliberative_workshops.pdf (accessed 11 August 2020).

Overton, L. and Fox O'Mahony, L. (2017) 'Understanding attitudes to paying for care among equity release customers: citizenship, solidarity and the "hardworking" homeowner', *Journal of Social Policy*, 46(1): 49–67.

Paine, T. (1987 [1797]) 'Agrarian justice', in M. Foot and I. Kramnick (eds) *The Thomas Paine Reader*, London: Penguin.

Parkinson, J.E., Kelly, G. and Gamble, A. (eds) (2001) *The Political Economy of the Company*, Oxford: Hart Publishing.

Parry, K. (2005) 'The Council Tax (New Valuation Lists for England) Bill. Research Paper 05/73, House of Commons Library'. Available at: www.parliament.uk/briefing-papers/rp05-73.pdf (accessed 4 June 2020).

Payne, G. and Williams, M. (2005) 'Generalization in qualitative research', *Sociology*, 39(2): 295–314.

Pedersen, S. and Smithson, J. (2013) 'Mothers with attitude – how the Mumsnet parenting forum offers space for new forms of femininity to emerge online', *Women's Studies International Forum*, 38: 97–106.

Pensions Regulator (2014) 'Automatic enrolment. Commentary and analysis: April 2013–March 2014'. Available at: https://webarchive.nationalarchives.gov.uk/20150105203841/http://www.thepensionsregulator.gov.uk/docs/automatic-enrolment-commentary-analysis-2014.pdf (accessed 13 August 2020).

Pensions Regulator (2017) Opting out: How to process 'opt-outs' from workers who want to leave a pension scheme. Available at: www.thepensionsregulator.gov.uk/-/media/thepensionsregulator/files/import/pdf/detailed-guidance-7.ashx (accessed 17 August 2020).

Pensions Regulator (2019) 'Earnings thresholds'. Available at: www.thepensionsregulator.gov.uk/en/employers/new-employers/im-an-employer-who-has-to-provide-a-pension/declare-your-compliance/ongoing-duties-for-employers-/earnings-thresholds (accessed 18 November 2019).

Percy, A. (2017) 'Universal public services: a larger life for the ordinary person', in Social Prosperity Network (ed) *Social Prosperity for the Future: A Proposal for Universal Basic Services*, London: Institute for Global Prosperity, University College, pp 9–16. Available at: www.ucl.ac.uk/bartlett/igp/sites/bartlett/files/universal_basic_services_-_the_institute_for_global_prosperity_.pdf (accessed 4 June 2020).

Pettit, P. (1997) *Republicanism: A Theory of Freedom and Government*, Oxford: Oxford University Press.

Piachaud, D. (2018) 'Basic income: confusion, claims and choices', *Journal of Poverty and Social Justice*, 26(3): 299–314.

Pierson, P. (1994) *Dismantling the Welfare State? Reagan, Thatcher and the Politics of Retrenchment*, Cambridge: Cambridge University Press.

Piketty, T. (2014) *Capital in the 21st Century*, Cambridge, MA: Harvard University Press.

Plimmer, F. (1999) 'The council tax: the need for a revaluation', *Journal of Property Tax Assessment and Administration*, 5: 27–39.

Portes, J. (2017) 'Universal basic services', in Social Prosperity Network (ed) *Social Prosperity for the Future: A Proposal for Universal Basic Services*, London: Institute for Global Prosperity, University College, pp 17–27. Available at: https://ubshub.files.wordpress.com/2018/03/social-prosperity-network-ubs.pdf (accessed 4 June 2020).

Rawls, J. (1971) *A Theory of Justice*, Cambridge, MA: Harvard University Press.

Reed, H. and Percy, A. (2017) 'Technical appendix II. Shelter & food basic income supplement local governance UK budget effects', in Social Prosperity Network (ed) *Social Prosperity for the Future: A Proposal for Universal Basic Services*, London: Institute for Global Prosperity, University College, pp 41–55. Available at: www.ucl.ac.uk/bartlett/igp/sites/bartlett/files/universal_basic_services_-_the_institute_for_global_prosperity_.pdf (accessed 4 June 2020).

Rhenman, E. (1967) *Industrial Democracy and Industrial Management: A Critical Essay on the Possible Meanings and Implications of Industrial Democracy*, London: Tavistock.

Rinaldi, A. (2011) 'Pension awareness and nation-wide auto-enrolment: the Italian experience', Center for Research on Pensions and Welfare Policies, Working Paper 104/11. Available at: www.cerp.carloalberto.org/wp-content/uploads/2011/02/wp_104.pdf (accessed 4 June 2020).

Ring, P.J. (2012) 'Trust: a challenge for private pension policy', *Journal of Comparative Social Welfare*, 28(2): 119–28.

Robeyns, I. (2005) 'The capability approach: a theoretical survey', *Journal of Human Development*, 6(1): 93–117.

Robeyns, I. (2016) 'Capabilitarianism', *Journal of Human Development and Capabilities*, 17(3): 397–414.

Rogers, C. and Clarke, C. (2016) 'Mainstreaming social finance: the regulation of the peer-to-peer lending marketplace in the United Kingdom', *British Journal of Politics and International Relations*, 18(4): 930–45.

Ron, A. (2008) 'Visions of democracy in "Property-owning democracy": Skelton to Rawls and beyond', *History of Political Thought*, 29(1): 168–87.

Ronald, R. and Doling, J. (2012) 'Testing home ownership as the cornerstone of welfare: lessons from East Asia for the West', *Housing Studies*, 27(7): 940–61.

Ronald, R., Lennartz, C. and Kadi, J. (2017) 'What ever happened to asset-based welfare? Shifting approaches to housing wealth and welfare security', *Policy & Politics*, 45(2): 173–93.

Rowlingson, K. and McKay, S. (2013) 'Financial inclusion annual monitoring report 2013'. Available at: www.birmingham.ac.uk/Documents/college-social-sciences/social-policy/CHASM/2013/Financial-inclusion-report-2013-final.pdf (accessed 4 June 2020).

Rowlingson, K. and McKay, S. (2014) 'Financial inclusion annual monitoring report 2014'. Available at: www.birmingham.ac.uk/Documents/college-social-sciences/social-policy/CHASM/annual-reports/chasm-annual-monitoring-report-2014.pdf (accessed 4 June 2020).

Rowlingson, K. and McKay, S. (2015) 'Financial inclusion annual monitoring report 2015'. Available at: www.birmingham.ac.uk/Documents/college-social-sciences/social-policy/CHASM/annual-reports/chasm-financial-inclusion-monitoring-report-2015.pdf (accessed 4 June 2020).

Rowlingson, K. and McKay, S. (2016) 'Financial inclusion annual monitoring report 2016'. Available at: www.birmingham.ac.uk/ Documents/college-social-sciences/social-policy/CHASM/annual-reports/financial-inclusion-monitoring-report-2016.pdf (accessed 4 June 2020).

Rowlingson, K., Appleyard, L. and Gardner, J. (2016) 'Payday lending in the UK: regul(aris)ation of a necessary evil?', *Journal of Social Policy*, 45(3): 527–43.

Salignac, F., Muir, K. and Wong, J. (2016) 'Are you really financially excluded if you choose not to be included? Insights from social exclusion, resilience and ecological systems', *Journal of Social Policy*, 45(2): 269–86.

Sane, R. and Halan, M. (2017) 'Misled and mis-sold: financial misbehaviour in retail banks', *Journal of Comparative Economics*, 45(3): 429–44.

Santos, A. (2017) 'Cultivating the self-reliant and responsible individual: the material culture of financial literacy', *New Political Economy*, 22(4): 410–22.

Schneider, W. and Shiffrin, R.M. (1977) 'Controlled and automatic human information processing: I. Detection, search and attention', *Psychological Review*, 84(1): 1–66.

Schreiner, M., Clancy, M. and Sherraden, M. (2002) 'Saving performance in the American dream demonstration. A national demonstration of Individual Development Accounts'. Available at: www.microfinance.com/English/Papers/IDAs_in_ADD_Final_Report.pdf (accessed 28 May 2020).

Scottish Executive (2005) *Financial Inclusion Action Plan: Part of the Scottish Executive's Closing the Opportunity Gap to Tackling Poverty*, Edinburgh: Scottish Executive.

Scottish Widows (2020) Retirement report 2020. Available at: https:// adviser.scottishwidows.co.uk/assets/literature/docs/23829.pdf (accessed 13 August 2020).

Select Committee on Treasury (2003) *Providing Child Trust Fund Accounts*, London: House of Commons.

Sen, A.K. (1985) *Commodities and Capabilities*, Amsterdam: Elsevier.

Sen, A.K. (1992) *Inequality Reexamined*, New York: Russell Sage Foundation.

Sen, A.K. (1998) *Development as Freedom*, New York: Knopf Press.

Sen, A.K. (2009) *The Idea of Justice*, London: Allen Lane.

Serafino, P. (2019) 'Exploring the UK's digital divide'. Available at: www.ons.gov.uk/peoplepopulationandcommunity/householdcharacteristics/homeinternetandsocialmediausage/articles/exploringtheuksdigitaldivide/2019-03-04 (accessed 29 April 2020).

Sherraden, M. (1990) 'Stakeholding: Notes on a theory of welfare based on assets', *Social Service Review*, 64(4): 580–601.

Sherraden, M. (1991) *Assets and the Poor. A New American Welfare Policy*, New York: M.E. Sharpe.

Sherraden, M. (2003) 'Assets and the social investment state', in W. Paxton (ed) *Equal Shares? Building a Progressive and Coherent Asset-based Welfare Policy*, London: Institute for Public Policy Research, pp 28–41.

Simon, H.A. (1955) 'A behavioural model of rational choice', *Quarterly Journal of Economics*, 69(1): 99–118.

Skelton, N. (1924) *Constructive Conservatism*, London: William Blackwood and Sons.

Smith, S.J. (2008) 'Owner-occupation: at home with a hybrid of money and materials', *Environment and Planning A*, 40(3): 520–35.

Soaita, A.M. and Searle, B. (2016) 'Debt amnesia: homeowners' discourses on the financial costs and gains of homebuying', *Environment and Planning A*, 48(6): 1087–106.

Soaita, A.M., Searle, B.A., McKee, K. and Moore, T. (2017) 'Becoming a landlord: strategies of property-based welfare in the private rental sector in Great Britain', *Housing Studies*, 32(5): 613–37.

Social Prosperity Network (ed) (2017) *Social Prosperity for the Future: A Proposal for Universal Basic Services*, London: Institute for Global Prosperity, University College.

Standing, G. (2011) 'Responding to the crisis: economic stabilisation grants', *Policy & Politics*, 39(1): 9–25.

Standing, G. (2019) 'Basic income as common dividends: piloting a transformative policy. A report for the Shadow Chancellor of the Exchequer'. Available at: www.progressiveeconomyforum.com/wp-content/uploads/2019/05/PEF_Piloting_Basic_Income_Guy_Standing.pdf (accessed 13 September 2019).

Standing, G. (2020) 'Coronavirus has shown us why we urgently need to make a basic income a reality'. Available at: www.weforum.org/agenda/2020/04/coronavirus-made-basic-income-vital/ (accessed 22 April 2020).

Stanley, L., Deville, J. and Montgomerie, J. (2016) 'Digital debt management: the everyday life of austerity', *New Formations*, 87: 64–82.

StatsWales (2016) 'Average band D council tax, by billing authority'. Available at: https://statswales.gov.wales/Catalogue/Local-Government/Finance/Council-Tax/Levels (accessed 4 June 2020).

Stebbing, A. and Spies-Butcher, B. (2016) 'The decline of a homeowning society? Asset-based welfare, retirement and intergenerational equity in Australia', *Housing Studies*, 31(2): 190–207.

Stephens, M. (2001) 'Building society demutualisation in the UK', *Housing Studies*, 16(3): 335–52.

Stewart, D.W., Shamdasani, P.N. and Rook, D.W. (2007) *Focus Groups*, London: Sage.

Stoney, C. and Winstanley, D. (2001) 'Stakeholding: confusion or utopia? Mapping the conceptual terrain', *Journal of Management Studies*, 38(5): 603–26.

Storchi, S. and Johnson, S. (2016) 'Financial capability for wellbeing: an alternative perspective from the capability approach', *Bath Papers in International Development and Wellbeing*, No. 44, Centre for Development Studies, University of Bath.

Susskind, D. (2020a) 'Universal basic income is an affordable and feasible response to coronavirus'. Available at: www.ft.com/content/927d28e0-6847-11ea-a6ac-9122541af204 (accessed 7 September 2020).

Susskind, D. (2020b) *A World without Work: Technology, Automation and How We Should Respond*, London: Allen Lane.

Thaler, R. and Benartzi, S. (2004) 'Save More Tomorrow: using behavioral economics to increase employee saving', *Journal of Political Economy*, 112(1): S164–S187.

Thaler, R. and Benartzi, S. (2007) *The Behavioral Economics of Retirement Savings Behavior*, Washington, DC: American Association of Retired Persons Public Policy Institute.

Thaler, R. and Sunstein, C. (2008) *Nudge: Improving Decisions about Health, Wealth and Happiness*, New Haven, CT: Yale University Press.

Thurley, D. (2019) 'Pensions: automatic enrolment – current issues', House of Commons Library Briefing Paper. Available at: https://researchbriefings.parliament.uk/ResearchBriefing/Summary/SN06417 (accessed 19 November 2019).

Toussaint, J. and Elsinga, M. (2009) 'Exploring "housing asset-based welfare". Can the UK be held up as an example for Europe?', *Housing Studies*, 24(5): 669–92.

UK Finance (2019) 'UK payments markets summary 2019'. Available at: www.ukfinance.org.uk/sites/default/files/uploads/pdf/UK-Finance-UK-Payment-Markets-Report-2019-SUMMARY.pdf (accessed 30 April 2020).

United Nations Development Programme (2018) 'Human development indices and indicators. 2018 statistical update'. Available at: http://hdr.undp.org/sites/default/files/2018_human_development_statistical_update.pdf (accessed 14 August 2019)

Valuation Office Agency (2005) 'Council tax Wales revaluation. Post evaluation review of the operational aspects of the project'. Available at: https://webarchive.nationalarchives.gov.uk/20141002132556/http://www.voa.gov.uk/corporate/_downloads/pdf/ctRevalWales_2005_ProjectEvaluation.pdf (accessed 4 June 2020).

Valuation Office Agency (2015) 'Council tax band changes due to 2005 revaluation in Wales'. Available at: www.gov.uk/government/publications/properties-changing-council-tax-band-as-a-result-of-the-2005-revaluation-in-wales (accessed 4 June 2020).

Van de Ven, J. (2012) 'Implications of the National Employment Savings Trust for vulnerable sectors of the UK labour market: a reduced-form statistical evaluation', *National Institute Economic Review*, 219: 77–89.

Van der Zwan, N. (2014) 'Making sense of financialisation', *Socio-Economic Review*, 12(1): 99–129.

Van Parijs, P. (1991) 'Why surfers should be fed: the liberal case for an unconditional basic income', *Philosophy & Public Affairs*, 20(2): 101–31.

Van Parijs, P. (1997) *Real Freedom for All, What (If Anything) Can Justify Capitalism?*, Oxford: Clarendon Press.

Van Parijs, P. and Vanderborght, Y. (2017) *Basic Income: A Radical Proposal for a Free Society*, Cambridge, MA: Harvard University Press.

Walks, A. (2016) 'Homeownership, asset-based welfare and the neighbourhood segregation of wealth', *Housing Studies*, 31(7): 755–84.

Watson, M. (2008) 'Constituting monetary conservatives via the "savings habit": New Labour and the British housing market bubble', *Comparative European Politics*, 6(3): 285–304.

Watson, M. (2009) 'Planning for the future of asset-based welfare? New Labour, financialized economic agency and the housing market', *Planning, Practice and Research*, 24(1): 41–56.

Watson, M. (2010) 'House price Keynesianism and the contradictions of the modern investor subject', *Housing Studies*, 25(93): 413–26.

Welsh Government (2002a) *Freedom and Responsibility in Local Government: A Policy Statement from the Welsh Assembly Government. March 2002*, Cardiff: Welsh Government.

Welsh Government (2002b) *Council Tax Revaluation and Rebanding 2005: A Consultation Paper from the Welsh Assembly Government, December 2002*, Cardiff: Welsh Government.

Welsh Government (2003) *Council Tax Revaluation and Rebanding 2005: Decisions and Revised Proposals for New Valuation Bands. A Supplementary Consultation Paper for the Welsh Assembly Government*, Cardiff: Welsh Government.

Welsh Government (2004a) *Council Tax Revaluation and Rebanding 2005*, Cardiff: Welsh Government.

Welsh Government (2004b) 'Working group on local government financial statistics: note by the National Assembly for Wales council tax revaluation in Wales'. Available at: http://webarchive.nationalarchives. gov.uk/20140505104649/http://www.local.communities.gov.uk/ finance/stats/wglfs/wglfs-04-08.pdf (accessed 5 June 2020).

Welsh Government (2004c) *Council Tax Revaluation and Rebanding 2005: Transitional Arrangements Consultation Paper*, Cardiff: Welsh Government.

Welsh Government (2005a) 'Note by the Welsh Assembly Government: revaluation of council tax in Wales, WGLGFS (05)12'. Available at: http://webarchive.nationalarchives.gov.uk/20140505104649/ http://www.local.communities.gov.uk/finance/stats/wglfs/wglfs-05-12.pdf (accessed 5 June 2020).

Welsh Government (2005b) 'Submission to the Lyons inquiry into local government: annex B'. Available at: www.assemblywales.org/ N0000000000000000000000000042136.pdf (accessed 4 June 2020).

Welsh Government (2008) *Local Authorities to Get Helping Hand to Provide Extra Support for Children in Care*, 14 May, Cardiff: Welsh Government.

Welsh Government (2009a) *Assembly Government Reaches Child Trust Fund Account Target*, 12 May, Cardiff: Welsh Government.

Welsh Government (2009b) 'Taking everyone into account: financial inclusion strategy for Wales'. Available at: http://resources.hwb.wales. gov.uk/VTC/2009-10/financial-education/finance-education-v2/ documents/FinInclDoc.pdf (accessed 5 June 2020).

Welsh Government (2016) 'Financial inclusion strategy for Wales 2016'. Available at: https://gov.wales/sites/default/files/publications/ 2018-11/money-and-financial-inclusion-strategy_0.pdf (accessed 4 June 2020).

Welsh Government (2020) 'Curriculum for Wales guidance'. Available at: https://hwb.gov.wales/storage/331eb63b-481f-4b0b-a607-5e6c3e41ae0f/curriculum-for-wales-guidance-070220.pdf (accessed 17 February 2020).

Western Mail (2005) 'Safe as houses? Council tax is a key election issue', 23 April.

Westlake, A. (2011) 'The UK poverty rip-off. The poverty premium 2010'. Available at: https://resourcecentre.savethechildren.net/node/13400/pdf/uk-poverty-rip-off-poverty-premium.pdf (accessed 22 October 2019).

White, S. (2003) *The Civic Minimum: On the Rights and Obligations of Economic Citizenship*, Oxford: Oxford University Press.

White, S. (2010) 'A modest proposal? Basic capital versus higher education subsidies', *British Journal of Politics and International Relations*, 12(1): 37–55.

White, S. (2011) 'Basic income versus basic capital: can we resolve the disagreement?', *Policy & Politics*, 39(1): 67–81.

White, S. (2015) 'Basic capital in the egalitarian toolkit?', *Journal of Applied Philosophy*, 32(4): 417–31.Whitehead, C. (2010) 'Shared ownership and shared equity: reducing the risks of home-ownership?'. Available at: http://citeseerx.ist.psu.edu/viewdoc/download?doi=10.1.1.471.771&rep=rep1&type=pdf (accessed 4 June 2020).

Whitehead, C. and Monk, S. (2011) 'Affordable home ownership after the crisis: England as a demonstration project', *International Journal of Housing Markets and Analysis*, 4(1): 326–40.

Whitehead, C., Travers, T. and Kielland, T. (2006) *A Stake in the Future. Equity Stakes and Landlord Savings Plans*, London: London Councils.

Wijburg, G. (2019) 'Privatised Keynesianism and the state-enhanced diversification of credit: the case of the French housing market', *International Journal of Housing Policy*, 19(2): 143–64.

Wilkinson, T.M. (2013) 'Nudging and manipulation', *Political Studies*, 61: 341–55.

Willetts, D. (2010) *The Pinch: How the Baby Boomers Took Their Children's Future – and Why They Should Give It Back*, London: Atlantic.

Williams, C. and Mooney, G. (2008) 'Decentring social policy? Devolution and the discipline of social policy: a commentary', *Journal of Social Policy*, 37(3): 489–507.

Williamson, D. (2009) 'Labour and Plaid rule out council tax revaluation'. Available at: www.walesonline.co.uk/news/wales-news/labour-plaid-rule-out-council-1879339 (accessed 4 June 2020).

Willis, L.E. (2008) 'Against financial literacy education', *Iowa Law Review*, 94(1): 197–285.

Willis, L.E. (2011) 'The financial education fallacy', *American Economic Review*, 101(3): 429–34.

Willis, L.E. (2013) 'When nudges fail: slippery defaults', *University of Chicago Law Review*, 80(3): 1155–229.

Women's Budget Group (2010) 'A gender impact assessment of the Coalition government budget, June 2010'. Available at: https://wbg.org.uk/wp-content/uploads/2016/12/RRB_Reports_12_956432831.pdf (accessed 4 June 2020).

World Bank (2014) 'Global financial development report. Financial inclusion 2014'. Available at: https://openknowledge.worldbank.org/handle/10986/16238 (accessed 4 June 2020).

Index

loss aversion 36, 39
low-income groups 9, 124
Luo, G. 79
Lusardi, A. 26, 34
Lusardi et al 36
Lyons, M. 100

M

MacIntyre, K. 68
Maclennan, D. 82
Madrian, B.C. 41
manipulation 40
Marquand, D. 30
Marron, D. 2, 7
Marshall, T.H. 30
Martinelli, L. 124
material inequality 3
McIntosh, I. 17–18
McKay, S. 4
McKillop et al 58–9
McQuaid, R. 33
Meade, J.E. 79
Means, G. 120
Miao, J. 82
microfinance 119
middle-class consumers 9
millennials 82–5
mindset 29
Mirrlees et al 97–8, 99, 100
mis-selling scandals 18–19
Mitchell, O. 26
mobile phones 16, 119
money 34, 43, 87, 111, 114, 116
Money Advice Service 8, 27, 28, 29
Money & Pensions Service 112
Money Saving Expert 118
Montalban, M. 118
Montgomerie, J. 118, 120
Mooney, G. 54, 55–6
More, Thomas 88
Morgan, Rhodri 55, 57
mortgages 19, 25, 72, 74–5
Muir, K. 9, 13–14
Mumsnet 118
mutuals 122–3

N

Nam, Y. 48
National Child Development
 Survey 51
National Employment Savings Trust
 (NEST) 62
National Health Service
 (NHS) 91, 125
need satisfiers 93
negative freedom 32
negative liberty 12

neoliberalism 7, 8, 12, 20–2, 74,
 118, 120
neoliberals 85
neutrality 99
New Zealand 62
Nissan, D. 51
no-interest loan schemes 5
Northern Ireland 115
*Nudge: Improving Decisions about Health,
 Wealth and Happiness* (Thaler and
 Sunstein) 36
nudging 37–8, 39–40, 41
Nussbaum, Martha 31

O

O'Donnell, N. 25
OECD 27, 28, 29
Office for Budget Responsibility 123
Office for National Statistics
 (ONS) 125–6
Ofsted 113
Olin Wright, E. 90
online banking 125, 126
online forums 117–18
opt-outs 61, 62, 63, 64, 65, 66–7, 68
Osborne, George 46, 85
Overton, L. 80–1
ownership 81–2, 83, 85, 86, 122

P

Paine, Thomas 89–90
pandemic, COVID-19 123–5
parental support 14
Parkinson, J.E. 122
paternalism 39–40
payday lenders 10
payment accounts, basic 15, 16
Payment Accounts Directive 15
peer-to-peer lending 117
Pension Wise 90
pensions 6, 18, 20, 38–9, 90, 110
 and automatic enrolment 4, 7, 23,
 41–2, 47, 59–69
Percy, A. 91, 95, 96
personal wealth 77
phones 16, 92, 119
physical distancing measures 124, 125
physical wealth 77
Pickles, Eric 106
Pierson, C. 79
Piketty, T. 80
*The Pinch: How the Baby Boomers
 Took Their Children's Future – and
 Why They Should Give It Back*
 (Willetts) 83–4
platform economy 118
policy action teams (PATs) 3